A World of Communities

Text by

Marcia S. Gresko

Editorial Advisors

John-Paul Bianchi

Deanna Washinsky

BLACKBIRCH PRESS, INC.

Woodbridge, Connecticut

Published by Blackbirch Press, Inc.
260 Amity Road
Woodbridge, CT 06525

Web site: www.blackbirch.com
Email: staff@blackbirch.com

©1998 Blackbirch Press, Inc.
First Edition

Printed in the United States

10 9 8 7 6 5 4 3 2 1

Table of Contents

Introduction

Imagine yourself in a jet plane flying around the world. It would take you about two days to circle the earth. During your trip you would see different kinds of landscapes. You'd see jagged mountains and flat **plains**. There'd be thousands of islands and lots and lots of water. You'd be too high up to see people. But you'd see great cities, small towns, and the checkerboard pattern of farms.

Most of the world's more than 6 billion people live on plains or in hilly regions. These areas usually have **fertile** (rich) soil and an excellent water supply. This makes them good areas for farming, manufacturing, and trade. Fewer people live in mountainous areas or in deserts. In places like these it is too hard to grow much food. The soil is often also poor and travel is hard.

WHERE PEOPLE LIVE AFFECTS *HOW* THEY LIVE. It affects the kinds of clothes people wear and the kinds of foods they eat. Think about what you are wearing right now. Why do your clothes look the way they do? Think about the food you had for dinner last night. How many of the foods were grown in an area near you? Are there any foods you know of that you have never had a chance to eat?

Where you live also affects how your house is built. What kind of home do you live in? Is the roof built to hold a lot of snow? Or do you live in a concrete house that keeps you cool year round?

In this book, you will learn about how people live all over the world. You will learn about people in India, China, Russia, South Africa, Israel, England, Puerto Rico, and the West Indies. You will also see how different the land and **climate** are around the world. As you learn these things, you'll begin to see why people in different lands have different clothes, food, and housing. For example, people who live in the warm climate of Puerto Rico wear light clothing. They eat lots of island-grown fruit and enjoy outdoor sports. People in frosty Russia wear heavy clothing almost all year round. They eat heavy, filling foods and enjoy indoor activities like going to the movies.

WHEREVER PEOPLE LIVE THEY ARE PART OF A COMMUNITY. In quiet, **rural** areas a community may be very small. Its people may all belong to the same religious and **ethnic groups**. Children may all attend the same school. Many families may even be related. But it's different in towns and cities (**urban** places). There, many people from all over live together. In a big city, people belong to many different kinds of communities at the same time.

PEOPLE IN COMMUNITIES ALL OVER THE WORLD ARE DIFFERENT IN MANY WAYS. They speak other languages. They celebrate other holidays. And they observe other religions. They also eat different kinds of foods and wear different kinds of clothing. They even dance and sing to different kinds of music.

BUT, PEOPLE IN COMMUNITIES ALL OVER THE WORLD ARE ALSO THE SAME IN MANY WAYS. People everywhere tell stories, celebrate holidays, and follow

A castle in the English countryside.

religions. They build homes, raise families, and try to educate their children. They work, play, and create arts and crafts.

LEARNING ABOUT COMMUNITIES AROUND THE WORLD IS IMPORTANT. It helps us understand how and why people are different from ourselves. Learning about others is a great way for us to better understand who we are, too!

Israeli children in Jerusalem.

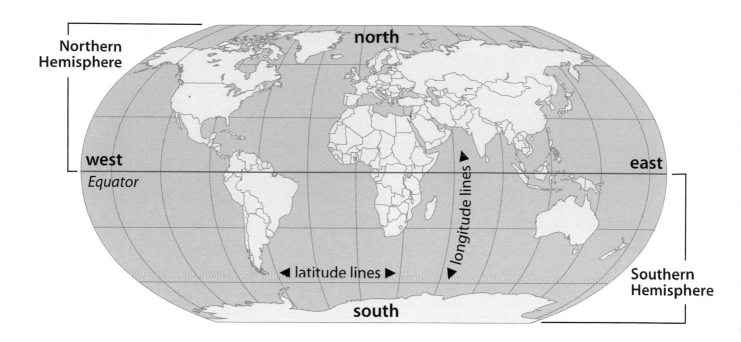

The World of Maps

What is the highest point in China? Where are South Africa's gold mines located? What is the capital of Russia? Where do most people in India live? The answers to all these questions can be found on maps.

A map is a carefully drawn picture of the earth or a part of the earth. Maps are important tools that give give us all kinds of information. Travelers use them to plan trips. Scientists use them to study the weather. Airplane pilots use them to find their way through fog and clouds. You have probably used maps yourself. Have you ever looked at a directory in the mall? Have you ever seen a drawing of how your school is laid out? Have you ever gotten a drawing of where the exhibits are in a museum? If you have done any of these things, you have used a map!

There are many kinds of maps. There are maps of your city, your state, your country, and your planet. There are even maps of the moon and maps of the ocean floor. A **topographical map** would help you find the highest point in China. It shows natural features—jungles, deserts, and mountains. Look at a **natural resources map** to locate South Africa's gold mines. To find the capital of Russia you would check a **political map**. It shows you capital cities, big cities, and the borders between countries. If you looked at a **population density map** you would see where most people in India live.

Maps can answer lots of questions, but you have to know how to read them. Maps use names and numbers. Some have special colors and shapes. Certain lines and little pictures all mean something special on a map.

Helpful Hint

Can't remember the 7 continents? Try to remember that 6 of the 7 begin and end with the letter "A." The seventh begins and ends with the letter "E." All the continents end with the same letter they begin with!

There are four important direction words on a map. **Direction** means "which way." **North** is the direction toward the North Pole. It is shown at the top of the map. **South** is toward the South Pole. It is shown at the bottom of the map. **East** is the direction where the sun rises each morning. It's on the right side of the map. **West** is the direction where the sun sets each evening. It's on the left side of the map. Most maps have a **compass** that shows these four directions.

You will see the word **equator** on most world maps. But, even if you flew all the way around the world, you would never actually see it. The equator is an imaginary line around the fat, middle part of the earth. It divides the earth into two equal parts. The **Northern Hemisphere** is above the equator. The **Southern Hemisphere** is below the equator. Many other imaginary lines appear on a map. Lines of **latitude** go around the world in the same direction as the equator (from left to right). You can tell how far north or south a place is by looking at them. Lines of **longitude** go around the world from the North Pole to the South Pole

(from top to bottom). They can tell you how far east or west a place is.

The **map legend** or **map key** helps you understand the colors, lines, and pictures you see on a map. For example, an airplane symbol might stand for an airport. The color green may show where forests are. On most maps a circle or dot indicates a major city. A star usually shows the location of a country's capital.

One other thing you can't help noticing about a map: It's mostly blue! That's because more than 70% of the earth's surface is covered by water. The Atlantic Ocean, the Pacific Ocean, the Indian Ocean, and the Arctic Ocean are earth's major bodies of water. These oceans separate huge land masses called **continents**. The seven continents are Asia, Africa, North America, South America, Antarctica, Europe, and Australia.

Key Map Terms

Equator: imaginary line around fat middle of Earth
Longitude: lines that go from top to bottom
Latitude: lines that go from left to right
Northern Hemisphere: above the equator
Southern Hemisphere: below the equator
Star symbol: capital city
Circle or dot: major city

India

Imagine yourself flying east from the United States, over the Atlantic Ocean. If you kept flying, you would fly over Europe and wind up in Asia. This is the huge **continent** that is home to India. It is also the continent that contains both China and Russia.

India is north of the **equator**. This means India is in the **Northern Hemisphere**. The country is shaped like a big piece of pizza. The pointy part, in the south, is surrounded by the Indian Ocean. The waters along India's western coast are called the Arabian Sea. The waters along India's eastern coast are called the Bay of Bengal.

Map Key
★ Capital City
● Major City

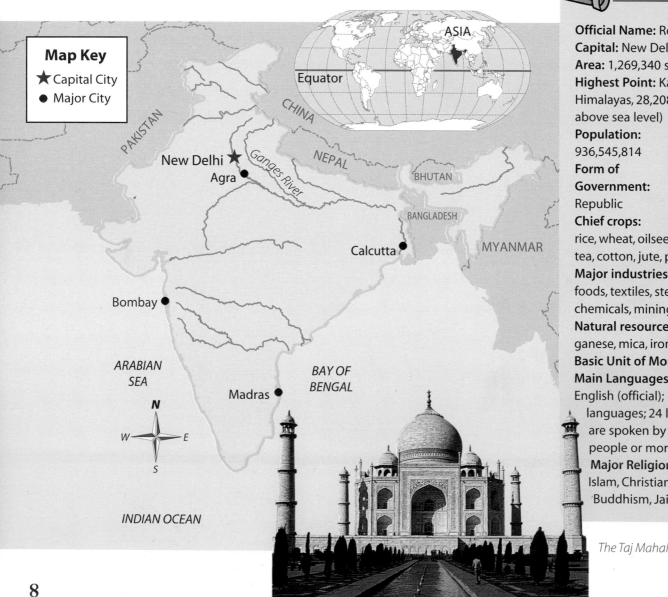

The Taj Mahal is in Agra.

At a Glance

Official Name: Republic of India
Capital: New Delhi
Area: 1,269,340 square miles
Highest Point: Kanchenjunga, Himalayas, 28,208 feet above sea level)
Population: 936,545,814
Form of Government: Republic

27% urban 73% rural

Population Distribution

Chief crops: rice, wheat, oilseeds, sugarcane, tea, cotton, jute, potatoes
Major industries: processed foods, textiles, steel, machinery, chemicals, mining
Natural resources: coal, manganese, mica, iron ore, bauxite
Basic Unit of Money: Rupee
Main Languages: Hindi and English (official); 14 other official languages; 24 languages that are spoken by a million people or more
Major Religions: Hinduism, Islam, Christianity, Sikhism, Buddhism, Jainism

India is about one third the land area of the United States. But three times more people live in India than in the United States. All together, more than 930 million people live in India.

The land of India is quite varied. In the northeast is the border with the country of Nepal. Here lie the Himalaya mountains. These are the world's highest mountains. Below the mountains, in the valleys, lies some of India's best farmland. There, flat **fertile** plains produce a rich variety of crops. In this region, the waters of the Ganges River flows. This is India's most important river. Because the soil is so rich and the water is so plentiful, the region near the Ganges is the most densely populated part of the country.

In the northwestern region of India is the border with Pakistan. Here, the land is quite different. The dry weather of the Thar Desert creates an environment unfit for most people. Hot, dry winds blow over sand dunes. There is no water, and little can grow.

All together, India has more than 4,350 miles of coastline. This has made fishing and trade two of the country's major **industries** (businesses). Some of India's most important business and industrial centers are located on the coast. India's business and industrial capital is the city of Bombay, located on the western coast.

India's Wealth: Who Owns What?
(ownership of items, per 1,000 people)

Think It Over:
How do you think this compares with your country?

Televisions	Cars	Telephones	VCRs	PCs
27	3	6	4	less than 1

Many fishing villages fill India's 4,350 miles of coastline.

The Many Communities of India

Like most very large countries, India's people are a mix of **ethnic groups**, religions, and social backgrounds. And, like you, each of India's people belongs to many different communities at the same time. Let's look at some of the different kinds of communities that can be found in India.

Ethnic Communities

There are three major ethnic groups in India. The largest group, which is nearly three-quarters of the population, is Indo-Aryan. Members of this group are of mixed **ancestry**. They are a mix of native Indian and white European races. Indo-Aryans most commonly speak English and Hindi.

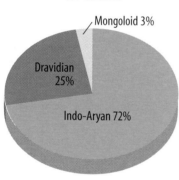

Ethnic Divisions of India

Mongoloid 3%
Dravidian 25%
Indo-Aryan 72%

The second-largest ethnic group, about a quarter of the population, is called Dravidian. This is a native Indian race. The most commonly spoken Dravidian languages are Tamil, Malayalam, Telugu, and Kannada.

The third major ethnic group in India is called Mongoloid. These people originated in other parts of Asia, mostly in China and Russia. About 3% of the population belongs to this group.

Religious Communities

The most common religion in India, is **Hindu**. Nearly 83% of the country's population is Hindu. Hindus worship many different gods and goddesses. The three most important gods are Vishnu, Shiva, and Brahma. The most important goddesses are Parvati and Lakshmi. Every Hindu home has at least one **shrine** to the gods. Most often, colorful flowers, beads, small statues, and incense decorate the shrines.

In a Hindu family, there is a special ceremony for boys between the ages of 8 and 12. Called the Thread Ceremony, this ritual marks a change from boyhood to manhood within the Hindu community. During the ceremony, the boy and his father stand next to a sacred fire. Then a sacred thread is placed on the boy's right shoulder. From that day forward, the boy will wear the thread every day of his life.

The second-biggest religion in India is **Islam**. **Muslims** (followers of Islam) make up about 11% of the population. Muslims pray to the god Allah. They learn from a holy book called the Koran. Islam was founded by Muhammad. He is believed to be Allah's **prophet**, or messenger.

Two other religions also play an important role in India's culture. They are Jainism and Sikhism (SEEK•izm). Jains believe in total nonviolence. They eat no meat. They even cover their mouths with cloths to prevent accidentally swallowing bugs.

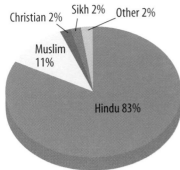

Major Religions of India

- Christian 2%
- Sikh 2%
- Other 2%
- Muslim 11%
- Hindu 83%

Young Hindu girls celebrate Diwali with sparklers.

At a Glance

Holidays and Festivals

★ **National Holidays**

Independence Day: August 15. Celebration of India's independence from Britain in 1947.

Republic Day: January 26. Marks the anniversary of the beginning of the Indian Republic in 1950. Elaborate parades feature highly decorated elephants and camels.

★ **Other Holidays**

Diwali: Hindu New Year celebration that comes at the end of October or beginning of November. Known as the "Fesitval of Lights."

Holi: Hindu festival held in February or March. Celebrates the coming of spring. People run through the streets splashing each other with colored water and powder.

Ramadan: A month-long period of prayer and fasting for Muslims.

Brainstorm
Are any of India's holidays similar to ones you celebrate?

Artistic and Cultural Communities

Indian art is influenced by religion. Famous landmarks include fabulous temples and huge statues of gods carved into cliff walls. Indian dancers use facial expressions and the positions of their hands, feet, and fingers to tell stories based on Indian myths and legends.

Traditional music is played on stringed instruments, drums, gongs, and flutes. Much is devoted to religious ideas. Plays come in many forms, such as puppet theater and dramatic masked productions. These, too, often present wonderful tales of gods and goddesses.

Daily Life

Daily life depends on where people live. About 73% of Indians live in **rural** (country-like) areas in small farming villages. Most of the rest live in cities and towns.

Educational Communities

Only about one in three of India's adults can read and write. Education is free for children ages 6 to 14. Children are expected to attend school, but not

Young girls work selling peanuts.

Brainstorm

There are celebrations that focus on the family in just about every culture on Earth. Can you think of any holidays or festivals that celebrate family in your country? Why do you think it is important to celebrate family ties?

everyone does. Most of India's children only go to school until the fifth grade.

Communities of Friends

Many children in India have responsibilities. Farm children help with chores such as taking care of the family's animals. In the cities, children may help in shops or with younger family members. Kids have responsibilities, but they enjoy being with friends. Children play traditional games such as chess, which began in India. Girls especially like to play Five Stones, a game similar to jacks. And, all over India, kids go to the movies. Even the smallest village usually has a movie screen and projector.

Family Communities

Family ties are very important in India. There is even a festival that celebrates the relationship between brothers and sisters. Sisters tie a decorated silk thread around their brothers' wrists. Then they place a red powder dot on their foreheads. Sisters also prepare sweet foods for their brothers to show their affection. Brothers give their sisters several gifts and promise to defend them.

Community Project

Making Mehandi Designs

Mehandi are flowery designs that are painted on women's hands and feet. Mothers often paint these designs on children for the Diwali festival and for weddings and special occasions.

Materials

- Water-based paints and brushes
- Water-based magic markers

Directions

- Look at the designs on the hands below.

- Practice drawing or painting designs on a piece of paper. (Use designs shown here or make your own "Indian" designs.)
- OPTIONAL: Paint Mehandi designs on your classmates' hands.

Bombay

Bombay is one of India's most exciting cities. It is the country's commercial capital. More people want to live and work in Bombay than any other city in India.

In many of India's cities, **poverty** and overcrowding are huge problems. More than half of Bombay's 9.9 million people live in **slums**. The people who live in Bombay's slums have no running water or electricity. In some buildings, as many as 10 people may share one room. As many as 100 may share one toilet.

Not all of Bombay is poor. Because there is so much industry and business, the city also has great wealth. There are rich families with huge homes in the city's **suburbs** (outlying areas). They have

Bombay is India's most crowded city.

air-conditioning, fancy cars, microwaves, computers, and many servants.

One of the biggest businesses in Bombay is the movie industry. In fact, India has the biggest movie industry in the world! Because so many movies are made in Bombay, the city has been nick-named "Bollywood." Indians from all

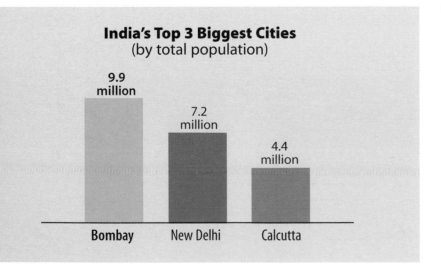

India's Top 3 Biggest Cities
(by total population)

9.9 million

7.2 million

4.4 million

Bombay   New Delhi   Calcutta

backgrounds share a love of movies. Walking down the crowded, noisy streets of Bombay, you would probably see at least one movie being made.

Brainstorm

1. What do you think it would be like to live in Bombay?

2. Do you live in a place that is very crowded or very private?

3. How do you think Bombay is similar to the big cities you know?

Geography Skill Builder

Look at the western coast on the India map on page 8. Can you find Bombay? Can you think of reasons why Bombay has become such a successful city for business?

Daily Life in Bombay

The city of Bombay is made up of many different sections. Near the water it has beaches. In the center of town, there are high-rise office buildings. On the city's outskirts, families live in many different kinds of neighborhood communities.

Women buy coconuts and flowers at one of Bombay's many open-air markets.

Two children sit on the steps of their home on the outskirts of Bombay.

China

China is slightly larger than the United States.

If you look at a map of the world, it is easy to find China. China is the third-largest country in the world. It takes up most of the eastern part of the **continent** of Asia. Only Russia (also located in Asia) and Canada are bigger.

China is north of the **equator**. That means China is in the **Northern Hemisphere**. The country is shaped like a huge rooster. Its head is in the east. Its fan-like tail is in the west. China is so big it shares its borders with more than 12 countries! That is more borders than most other countries of the world. Almost all of China's eastern

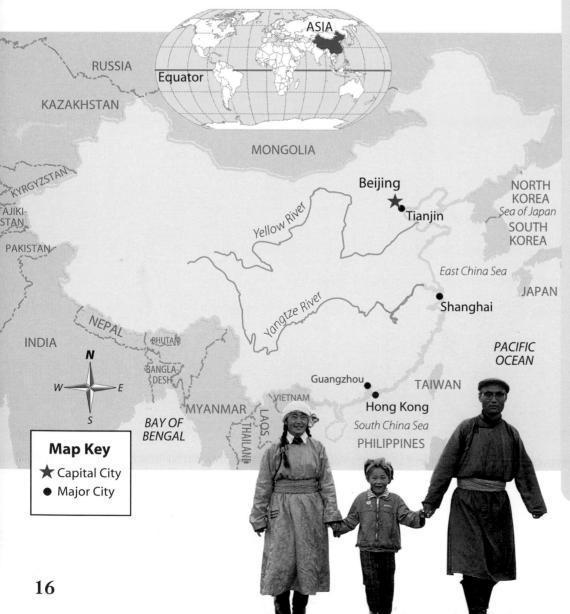

At a Glance

Official Name: People's Republic of China
Capital: Beijing
Area: 3,705,392 square miles
Highest Point: Mt. Everest, Himalayas (29,028 feet above sea level)
Population: 1,203,097,268
Form of Government: Communist state

29% urban
71% rural
Population Distribution

Chief crops: grain, rice, cotton, potatoes, tea
Major industries: iron, steel, coal, textiles and apparel, machinery and equipment, weapon systems
Natural resources: coal, iron ore, petroleum, mercury, tin, world's largest hydropower potential
Basic Unit of Money: Yuan
Main Languages: Standard Chinese or Mandarin
Major Religions: Daosim (Taoism), Buddhism, Islam, Christianity

Map Key
★ Capital City
● Major City

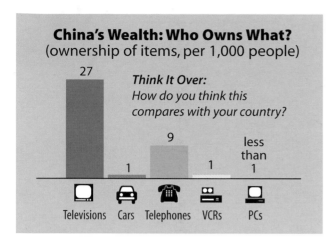

China's Wealth: Who Owns What?
(ownership of items, per 1,000 people)

Think It Over:
How do you think this compares with your country?

Televisions	Cars	Telephones	VCRs	PCs
27	1	9	1	less than 1

China has many different types of land. Its eastern regions are covered with flat, **fertile** plains and rolling hills. Two of the country's largest lakes are in the east. So are most of its 50,000 rivers. Also in this region are the country's two most important rivers, the Yangtze River and the Yellow River. Because of the rich soil and plentiful water, more than 90% of China's people live in the eastern half of the country. In the southwestern regions lie the icy Himalayas. This is the highest mountain range in the world. Mt. Everest, the world's highest peak, is located on the border of China and the country of Nepal. In China's northwestern regions are the dry environments of the Gobi and Taklimakan deserts. Also in the north is the famous 4,000-mile-long Great Wall. This human-made wonder is so huge it can even be seen from the moon!

border is along the Pacific Ocean. These waters include the Yellow Sea and the East and South China Seas. Off China's coast are many islands. Two of these islands are Taiwan and Hong Kong. The Chinese government considers both islands to be part of China.

In terms of people, China is the world's largest nation. One out of every five people in the world lives in China! More than 1.2 billion people live there.

The Great Wall of China

The Many Communities of China

About one third of China's population lives in **urban** (city) areas. Here, crowding, traffic, and pollution are major problems. About two thirds of China's people live in **rural** (country) areas. They work as farmers and have few modern conveniences. But no matter where they live, Chinese people belong to communities that include family, friends, neighbors, and many others.

Ethnic Communities

The largest ethnic group in China is the Han Chinese. More than 90% of the people are **descendants** of the Han. The Han were the earliest known people of central China. They ruled China for more than 400 years. Han Chinese speak Mandarin, the country's official language.

The rest of the Chinese people belong to one of the more than 50 different ethnic groups. Many have their own language, religion, dress, and way of life. Most ethnic Chinese live in communities far away from the cities.

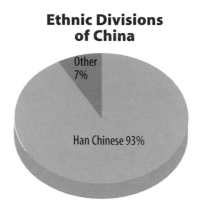

Ethnic Divisions of China

Other 7%

Han Chinese 93%

Religious Communities

Officially, the Chinese government discourages religious beliefs. That is because China is a **Communist** country. They feel religion stands in the way of the country's progress. Most Chinese are officially **atheist**, meaning they don't believe in any god.

Some young Chinese boys study to become Buddhist monks at an early age.

About 2% of the population follows traditional Chinese religious practices. These beliefs include many gods and a variety of magical practices. They also include worshipping **ancestors**. Other important ideas are drawn from Confucianism, Buddhism, and Taoism. Confucianism is based on the teachings of an important Chinese leader named Confucius. He taught the importance of family duty. He also taught the importance of kindness to others. Buddhism came to China from India about 2,000 years ago. Buddha taught that the soul is reborn many times on its way to becoming perfect. Taoism is based on the ideas of the teacher Lao Zi. It encourages people to live in harmony with nature.

Major Religions of China

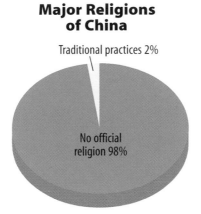

Traditional practices 2%

No official religion 98%

At a Glance

Holidays and Festivals

★ National Holidays

May Day: May 1. Also known as International Workers' Day. Honors working men and women around the world. Celebrated with family picnics, dancing, and fireworks.

National Day: October 1. Celebrates the formation of the People's Republic of China. There are speeches, parades, fireworks, and sporting events.

★ Other Holidays

New Year: Also known as the Spring Festival. Celebrated for five days in January or February. Special foods, fireworks, parades, and lion dancers are all part of the festivities.

Qing Ming: The "Feast of Pure Brightness" comes in April. People honor their dead relatives by bringing a picnic to the cemetery and cleaning grave sites.

Chinese New Year in Beijing

Mid-Autumn Feast: A harvest festival of thanksgiving. Round "moon-cakes" filled with a sweet sticky paste are eaten.

Note: You may have noticed that the Chinese use a lot of fireworks. That may be because fireworks (and gunpowder) were invented in China!

An actor from the Beijing Opera.

Artistic and Cultural Communities

China has a long history in the arts. Best-known, perhaps, are beautiful brush paintings that have been done for more than 2,000 years. The subjects traditionally come from nature. They include lovely landscapes of mountains, water, trees, or birds and flowers.

Paintings usually come with poems. These poems are written in a fine Chinese brush writing called **calligraphy**.

China has more than 300 different styles of opera. The best known is called Beijing Opera. Actors and actresses wear colorful make-up and fancy costumes. The colors stand for different personality **traits**. For example, red means bravery and black means strength.

There is an ancient craft-making tradition in China. Crafts-people make beautiful pottery called **porcelain**, embroidered silk, and items carved from jade.

Educational Communities

Educating China's huge population is a big job. Children in China attend school six days a week. They start school at the age of 6 or 7 and are required to go for at least six years. Chinese students learn many of the same subjects that you do, such as science and math. They also spend a lot of time learning to read and write the difficult Chinese language. Being a good **citizen** is very important to the Chinese people. Special classes encourage **patriotism**, or love of country. Politeness, honesty, and responsibility are also taught. Not every moment is spent at a desk, however. Physical exercise and team sports are also an important part of every school day.

Most children in China go to school until they are 13. Many students start middle school, but more than half drop out. Children who live in the country often leave to work in the fields or to find jobs to help their families.

Very few Chinese students go on to colleges. The entrance tests are hard, and there are not enough teachers or schools.

Chinese students attend school until they are 13 years old.

Brainstorm

How is your family like a Chinese family? How is it different? If you visited a Chinese family, what would you like to spend time doing with them?

Communities of Friends

The Chinese government has made rules to control China's huge population. One of these rules means Chinese couples are only allowed to have one child. But there is no shortage of children. Like you, Chinese children like to get together to play sports. They especially like playing ping pong, soccer, and basketball. You have to do some fancy footwork to win at the popular game called Kick-the-Bag. A small beanbag (like a hackysack) is kept in the air by kicking it with the inside of the heel. One person or a group can play.

Kites were **invented** in China. Flying them is always a popular pastime. There is even a kite-flying festival in April.

Family Communities

Family life has always been very important in China. Children are thought to be very special. Elderly family members are treated with great respect. Most young people live with their families until they get married, usually in their late 20's or early 30's. Divorce is uncommon in China.

Chinese families enjoy doing things together. Meals are always social occasions. Tasty Chinese cooking is known around the world! Family pets are popular in China, too. People in crowded cities keep birds, goldfish, and even crickets!

Community Project

Making Woodcuts

Like traditional Chinese paintings, woodcuts usually showed scenes from nature. They were made by carving a design into one side of a block of wood. The design was coated with ink and then the block pressed onto paper.

Materials

- clean foam meat trays
- dull pencils
- black tempera paint
- white paper

Directions

- Turn the foam tray over.
- Use the pencil to "carve" a simple design from nature like a flower, bird, tree, the sun, etc. into the surface of the bottom of the tray.
- Brush a thin layer of paint over the entire surface of your "block."
- Gently press the paper onto the design and smooth it lightly with your hand.
- Carefully lift the paper off.
- OPTIONAL: Trade designs with a classmate.

Guangzhou
(gwang•JO)

There are lots of reasons to visit Guangzhou. A large zoo, colorful markets, and fashionable shops make the city an exciting place. And, its delicious style of cooking is famous all over the world!

Eating in one of Guangzhou's many restaurants is a popular activity.

Guangzhou is located on the Pearl River Delta. The rich farmland in the region makes it perfect for growing rice. Rice is a main part of the Chinese diet.

Guangzhou's most important role is as a seaport. (The city was often called Canton by foreigners.) Guangzhou still hosts two giant business fairs every year. New Chinese products are shown. Thousands of business people from all over the world come to view them. The city is also a big manufacturing center. There are sugar refineries and large factories that make paper, chemicals, and machinery. Smaller factories produce craft articles such as jewelry and objects carved from jade and ivory.

Like most of China's large cities, Guangzhou is very crowded. People work in factories and businesses. Most people get around on bicycles. Families

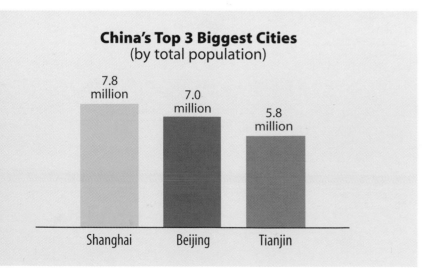

China's Top 3 Biggest Cities
(by total population)

7.8 million — Shanghai
7.0 million — Beijing
5.8 million — Tianjin

reindeer. On the eastern coast of Siberia is the Pacific Ocean. Eastern Siberia has mountains and active volcanoes. At its easternmost point, it is only 50 miles away from Alaska!

Brainstorm

1. What do you think it would be like to live in Siberia?
2. Do you live in a place where it is usually warm or usually cold?

Northern Siberia is mostly **tundra**. That is cold, barren, flat land. In the north, Siberia borders the Arctic Ocean. Freezing winters last eight months of the year. Few people live here. This is the homeland of the polar bear and the

Russia's Wealth: Who Owns What?
(ownership of items, per 1,000 people)

Think It Over:
How do you think this compares with your country?

Televisions	Cars	Telephones	VCRs	PCs
313	60	105	28	less than 1

Geography Skill Builder

Can you find the Bering Sea? That's what flows between Russia and Alaska.

West of the Ural Mountains is European Russia. This area is mostly a broad, flat, treeless **plain** called a **steppe**. Most Russians live in this area. Its **fertile** soil, milder weather, and rainfall make it good for farming.

Reindeer cross the tundra of northern Siberia.

Spreading across Russia's center from west to east is the world's largest evergreen forest. Lumbering is a major **industry**.

Russia has many large bodies of water and rivers. Travel by boat is an important means of **transportation**. Water also provides power to factories. The large fishing industry provides food for Russia's people.

The Many Communities of Russia

For a long time Russia's different groups worked together to make a modern country. Today, Russia is changing. Its communities are changing, too.

Ethnic Communities

Russia's approximately 150 million people come from many places. About 82% of people are of Russian **ancestry**. They come from a group of eastern European people called the Slavs. People in the slavic group speak Russian.

The second-largest **ethnic group** is the Tartars. These people came from Mongolia. They came to Russia as invaders more than 700 years ago. About 4% of the population belongs to this group.

The third-largest group is the Ukrainians. They make up about 3% of the population.

About 100 other ethnic groups make up the remaining 11% of the population. These groups observe different religions and **traditions**. Their lifestyles have little in common. Many speak their own language and use Russian as a second language. Sadly, these cultural differences have created problems. Several ethnic groups want to break away from Russia to form their own independent countries.

Ethnic Divisions of Russia

- Tartar 4%
- Ukrainian 3%
- Other 11%
- Russian 82%

Religious Communities

For years religious worship was discouraged by the government. Churches, mosques, and temples were closed. Many were destroyed or used in other ways. Religious holidays were replaced with **patriotic** holidays. Religious rituals for weddings, births, and deaths were not allowed. During this time, people observed their religious faiths in secret. Now, people are free to enjoy their holidays and customs.

The most common religion in Russia is Christianity. Most Christians belong to the Russian Orthodox Church. Their beliefs and practices are similar to those of the Catholic Church. Beautiful onion-shaped domes of the Russian Orthodox churches fill cities and towns all across the country.

The second-largest religion in Russia is **Islam**. Followers of this religion are called **Muslims**. They believe in one God, called Allah. Russia's Muslims live mostly in the areas that border central Asian countries.

The Jewish people have had a particularly difficult history in Russia. They were often the victims of violence. When the Soviet Union broke apart, many Jews decided to leave the country. Many traveled to the United States or Israel.

Artistic and Cultural Communities

Russia has a grand **heritage** in painting, building design, music, and dance.

The country is well known for its music and ballet. Many famous composers were Russian. Peter Tchaikovsky's ballets,

At a Glance

Holidays and Festivals

★**Political Holidays**

International Woman's Day: March 8. Honors women. Celebrated like Mother's Day in America.

Victory Day: May 9. Most popular holiday. Marks the end of World War II. Celebrated with parades and fireworks.

May Day: May 1. Celebrates the arrival of Spring. Honors working people.

★**Traditional Holidays**

Shrovetide (Butter Week): Celebrated for seven days at the beginning of Lent. Tricks, noise-making, carnivals, and costumes are common festivities. A straw figure of winter is burned and tasty filled pancakes called blini are eaten.

New Year's Day: Gifts are given and trees are decorated.

★**Religious Holidays**

Christmas and **Easter** are celebrated as they would be by Christians in other countries. Easter is the most important holiday in the Russian Orthodox year.

Brainstorm

If you were not allowed to celebrate a holiday, which one would you miss the most? Why?

Dancers perform at the world-famous Kirov Ballet in St. Petersburg.

Swan Lake, *The Nutcracker*, and *Sleeping Beauty*, are still popular the world over. They are performed often by the two great Russian dance companies, the Kirov and the Bolshoi.

Russia's different regional ethnic groups also have rich cultural traditions. Communities have their own styles of lively folk dancing, which they perform in different regional costumes.

Daily Life

Russia was part of the Soviet Union for almost 75 years. That was an organization of 14 **Communist** republics. Under communism, the government controlled every aspect of daily life. Housing, clothing, food, and transportation were cheap. School and health care were free. People were guaranteed jobs for life. But, the government told people how to lead their lives. Many freedoms were not allowed.

The Soviet Union broke up in 1991. Today Russia is changing quickly. It is moving toward **democracy** (rule by the people). In the process, there are many problems to be solved.

Educational Communities

Education is very important in Russia. School is free for all students. Children must go to school from the age of 6 until the age of 17. Most parents work full-time. Many children go to nursery schools.

Russian children go to school six days a week. Schoolwork is hard and classrooms are strict. Studying is taken very seriously, and weekly progress reports are usually sent home. Children often come in early or stay late to do their homework. Children with special talents in sports, music, dance, or mathematics may go to special schools.

After ninth grade, students can continue to go to a regular school or go to a trade school. Trade schools train students to work in farming or industry.

A young boy addresses his teacher in a Moscow classroom.

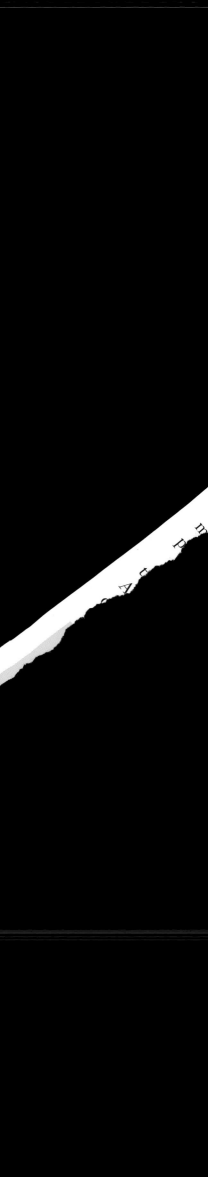

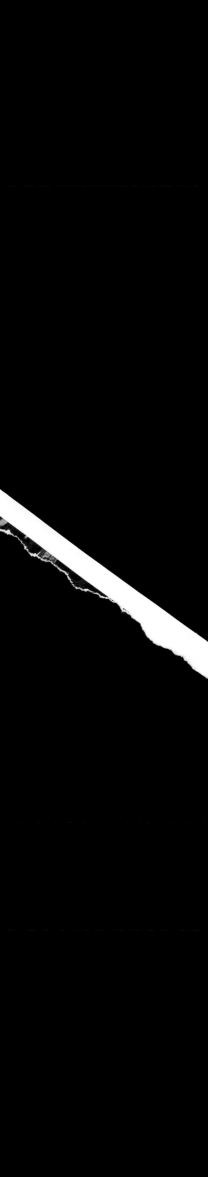

and other political events were often celebrated here.

All around the Kremlin area are many shops, modern offices, and cultural buildings. Moscow has a long history as the country's cultural center. There are almost 100 museums and art galleries. There are also more than 1,000 libraries! A symphony orchestra and the famous Bolshoi Theater Ballet company are also located there.

Manufacturing districts surround the commercial and cultural areas. Moscow is Russia's most important industrial city.

Most people get around Moscow on the **metro**, or subway. The Moscow metro probably has the fanciest train stations in the world! Each station is decorated in a different style. With their glass lighting fixtures and large, stone statues, they look like the splendid halls of a palace. Moscow is the transportation center of Russia. Highways and railways extend in all directions from the city into the countryside.

Sadly, like in many large cities, crime, pollution, and homelessness are big problems in Moscow.

Grand old buildings fill the streets of downtown Moscow.

South Africa

From its name, you can probably figure out where the country of South Africa is located. It is located at the southern tip of the huge **continent** of Africa. South Africa is south of the **equator**. That means it is in the **Southern Hemisphere**. Seasons for countries in the Southern Hemisphere are opposite to those in the **Northern Hemisphere**. When it is winter in the United States, it is summer in South Africa. South Africa shares its borders with the countries of Namibia, Botswana, Zimbabwe, Mozambique, and Swaziland in the north. The waters along South Africa's eastern coast are

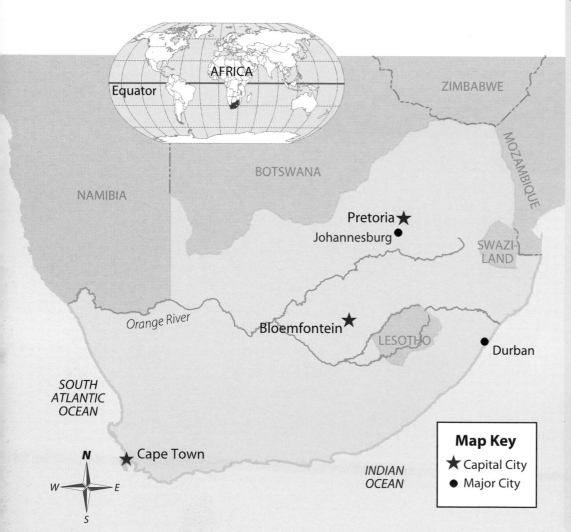

At a Glance

Official Name: Republic of South Africa

Capital: Pretoria (administrative); Cape Town (legislative); Bloemfontein (judicial)

Area: 471,444 square miles

Population: 45,095,459

Form of Government: Republic

Population Distribution: 50% rural, 50% urban

Chief crops: corn, grain, potatoes, sugar, fruit, tomatoes, tobacco

Major industries: gold, diamond, chrome mining, metalworking, food

Natural resources: gold, coal, iron ore, nickel, tin, uranium, gem diamonds, platinum, salt, natural gas, chromium

Basic Unit of Money: Rand

Main Languages: 11 official languages, including Afrikaans, English, Ndebele, Pedi, Sotho, Swazi, Tsonga, Tswana, Venda, Xhosa, Zulu

Major Religions: Christianity, Hinduism, Islam

Map Key
★ Capital City
● Major City

South Africa's Wealth: Who Owns What?
(ownership of items, per 1,000 people)

Think It Over:
How do you think this compares with your country?

101	95	146	21	less than 1
Televisions	Cars	Telephones	VCRs	PCs

called the Indian Ocean. The waters along the country's western coast are called the South Atlantic Ocean.

South Africa's land area is almost twice the size of Texas. About 45 million people live there.

Most of South Africa's land is a series of **plateaus** called **velds** (grassy plains) by South Africans. In the area named the High Veld is the world's largest and richest gold field. Gold, diamonds, and other metals are the country's most important natural resources. Many people work in mines and factories. South Africa gets little rain. This makes the land better for **grazing** animals than for farming. South Africa is one of the main sheep-raising and wool-producing countries in the

Brainstorm

Christmas and New Year's Day come during South Africa's summer. New Year's in South Africa is celebrated with barbecues, swimming, parades, and sporting events. How does your family celebrate New Year's Day? How are the activities you enjoy influenced by the climate of your area?

world. Giraffes, zebra, lions, rhinos, hippos, and elephants roam freely in protected wildlife parks.

The country's coastal areas are narrow. Along the western coast is the Namib Desert. The Kalahari Desert is located in the north.

The Many Communities of South Africa

For more than forty years, a government policy called **apartheid** (a-PAR-tide) was in place. This policy separated people in South Africa based on the color of their skin. Apartheid means "separateness" in the Afrikaans language. Apartheid laws told black people where they could live, and what jobs they could have. It even told them who they could marry. There were separate schools, restaurants, and other public places for whites and blacks.

Cape Town, in the south, is on the coast.

Nelson Mandela

Slowly, the South African government began changing the laws. Finally, in 1994, black South Africans voted for the very first time. Nelson Mandela became the first president of South Africa. He was a black leader who had spent 26 years in jail because he spoke out against apartheid.

Ethnic Communities

There are 4 major **ethnic groups** and 11 official languages in South Africa. The largest group—about three-quarters of the population—is Black or African. Different peoples make up this group. The largest of the groups is the Zulu. Other groups include the Xhosa and Sotho. Most Africans speak the language of their own group. Many Africans also speak English.

The second-largest ethnic group, about 14%, is white. White South Africans are divided into two groups. The majority are called Afrikaners. They are people whose **ancestors** came mostly from European lands: Netherlands, France, or Germany. They speak Afrikaans.

Zulu man

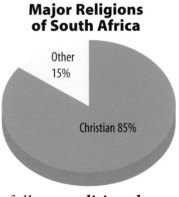

This language is a mixture of Dutch and phrases from other, mostly African, languages.

The third major ethnic group is called Colored. They are a mix of native African races, Asian peoples, and white European races. About 9% of people belong to this group. Most of them speak Afrikaans.

The last group is Indian. Indians make up 2% of the population. They usually speak English and Hindi.

Religious Communities

The most common religion in South Africa is Christianity. About 85% of the population is Christian. Whites, Coloreds, and more than half of Blacks attend a variety of Christian churches. About 25% of blacks follow **traditional** African religious beliefs, such as worshipping their ancestors. About 20% of blacks attend churches that combine Christianity with traditional African religious beliefs and practices.

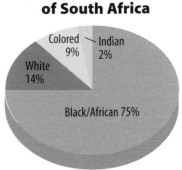

Ethnic Divisions of South Africa

- Colored 9%
- Indian 2%
- White 14%
- Black/African 75%

Major Religions of South Africa

- Other 15%
- Christian 85%

CndQTkcNChoKAAAADUlIRFIAAAAEAAAABAgGAAAAO

Hinduism, Buddhism, Judaism, and Islam are practiced by small groups of other South African **citizens**.

Artistic and Cultural Communities

Black South Africans have a rich **tradition** of folk arts and crafts. This artistic tradition focuses on adding color and beauty to objects used in everyday life. Some examples are pottery bowls, clothing, jewelry, and even homes.

Brainstorm

After apartheid ended, South Africa adopted a new flag. It now also has two national anthems. Why do you think it was important to make these changes? Can you think of anything in your country's history that was similar to apartheid?

Traditional music and dance combine song and storytelling. Instruments played are drums, pipes, and xylophones. The

At a Glance

Holidays and Festivals

★**National Holidays**

Freedom Day: April 27. Celebrates the official end of apartheid. A new constitution was approved. Black South Africans voted for the very first time.

★**Other Holidays**

Republic Day: May 31. Marks the decision by white South African voters to be a republic rather than a monarchy (ruled by king and queen).

New Year's Day: Celebrated as it is in the United States and other Western countries.

Christmas and Easter: Celebrated as it is in the United States and other Western countries.

Grahamstown Festival: Artists present music, theater, opera, and dance during this two week festival in July.

Nagmaal Festival: Afrikaner religious and social event. People come in from the farms to the cities and towns to go to

A woman celebrates Freedom Day.

church and visit with friends in what has become a "country fair-like" atmosphere.

Day of the Vow: December 16. Remembers a conflict between Zulu warriors and Afrikaner settlers.

Brainstorm

Apartheid created many problems for South Africa. Now that apartheid is over, there are many problems that need to be addressed. What do you think are some of the biggest problems facing South Africa today?

human voice is also used to imitate the sound of instruments.

Stories, folktales, and poems are told by one generation to the next. This is how people pass on their history and their most important customs.

Daily Life

Apartheid has ended, and the new government is working hard to make changes. But the quality of life for South Africa's people still depends a lot on the color of their skin.

Educational Communities

Until 1981, black children were not even required to go to school. The schools they went to were poor. Often, there was no heat or light, no books or supplies. White children went to schools that are similar to nice neighborhood schools in the United States.

Since the end of apartheid, schools are no longer separated (**segregated**) by law. All children between the ages of 7 and 16 are required to go to school. Education is free for the first five years. The new government hopes that it will be able to give all children ten years of free education by the end of the 1990s.

Communities of Friends

South Africans of all races love sports. The country's mild weather allows kids to play outside games and sports most of the year. Swimming is popular, and there are lots of pools open to all. Soccer is the favorite sport of most kids.

South Africa has only had television for the last 20 years. Watching television is now a popular way for friends to spend time. So is going to the movies.

Family Communities

About two thirds of all South Africans live in **urban** (city) areas. Most white

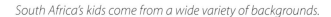
South Africa's kids come from a wide variety of backgrounds.

Community Project

Build a Zulu Kraal (Village)

Zulu houses are a unique art form. The traditional Zulu house is a bee-hive shaped grass hut. There are no windows and one arched doorway. The outside of the hut is often decorated with geometric shapes, patterns, and designs in bold colors.

Materials

- a six inch circle of tan construction paper
- a 2" x 12" strip of brown construction paper
- markers   • stapler

Directions

- Make a slit from the edge of the circle to its center. Overlap the edges to form a cone shaped roof.
- Cut an arched doorway in the middle of the brown paper.
- Decorate the brown strip of paper with geometric designs.
- Staple the end of the brown paper together to make the walls.
- Attach the roof to the walls with tape on the inside of the house.
- Arrange your Zulu house with your classmates to create a kraal.

families lead lives similar to those of middle-class Americans. They own a home. They have a nice car and can afford to take vacations. White adults still have the best jobs in government, business, and industry.

About half of black South Africans lead western-style lives in townships or cities. Still, many are poor. The other half live in **rural** areas called homelands. Most people in the homelands live the way their ancestors did. They make their living by farming. Houses are traditional cone-shaped dwellings made of mud, grass, and straw. Family life is difficult. Fathers often leave for long periods of time to earn money for their families in far away mines and factories. Sometimes they can only come home to see their families once or twice a year.

Johannesburg

Johannesburg is South Africa's second-largest city. It was founded more than 100 years ago when a rich gold field was discovered nearby. Today, Johannesburg is South Africa's leading center for industry and finance.

Like many of South Africa's cities, Johannesburg is modern. There are tall office buildings, shopping malls, and museums. There are art galleries, theaters, and peaceful parks. **Suburbs** are home to the city's wealthiest white people.

Almost half of Johannesburg's population works in the nearby gold mines.

Geography Skill Builder

South Africa has three capital cities. They are Pretoria, Capetown, and Bloemfontein. Can you find each of them on the map?

Downtown Johannesburg is crowded with shoppers and markets.

Schoolchildren in the township of Soweto learn to count.

Other people work in the city's many businesses and factories. Johannesburg's factories produce chemicals, machinery, furniture, and diamonds.

Fifteen miles outside Johannesburg is the township of Soweto. Townships were formed under apartheid. They provided housing for blacks who worked in cities but were not allowed to live there. Soweto has more than 2 million people, making it bigger than the city of Johannesburg. Soweto has a mixture of very poor areas and more well-to-do neighborhoods. There are modern schools, shopping centers, and open-air markets. But, much of Soweto and many

townships are still no more than large **slums**. They have cramped housing, no running water, and no electricity.

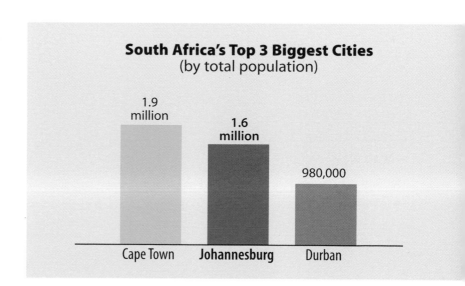

South Africa's Top 3 Biggest Cities
(by total population)

Cape Town: 1.9 million
Johannesburg: 1.6 million
Durban: 980,000

39

Israel

When you go to sleep at night in the United States, kids in Israel are just about waking up for school. That's because Israel is almost on the other side of the world. To get there by plane you would fly east from the United States. You would fly across the Atlantic Ocean, Europe, and the Mediterranean Sea. You would land on a part of the Asian **continent** called the Middle East. Israel is located on a thin piece of land where the continents of Europe, Asia, and Africa meet.

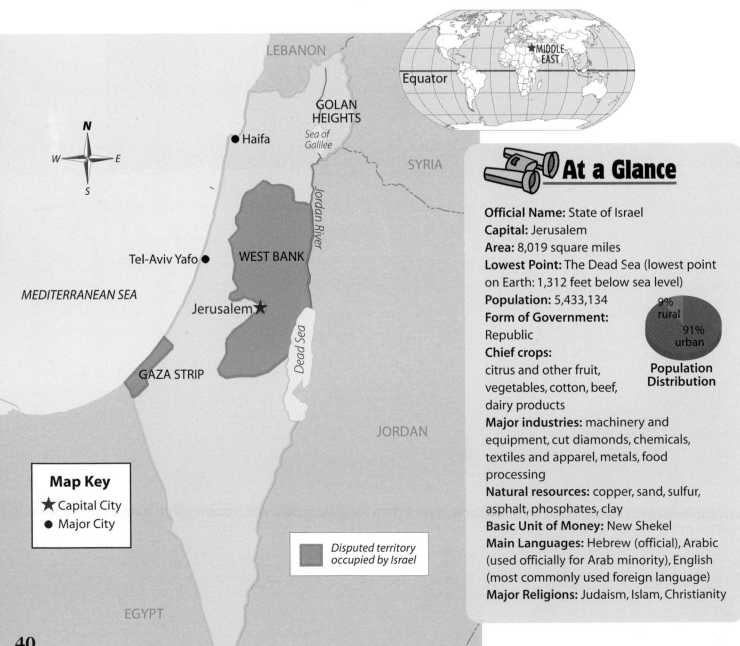

LEBANON

GOLAN HEIGHTS

Sea of Galilee

● Haifa

SYRIA

Jordan River

Tel-Aviv Yafo ●

WEST BANK

MEDITERRANEAN SEA

Jerusalem ★

Dead Sea

GAZA STRIP

JORDAN

EGYPT

★ MIDDLE EAST

Equator

Map Key
★ Capital City
● Major City

Disputed territory occupied by Israel

At a Glance

Official Name: State of Israel
Capital: Jerusalem
Area: 8,019 square miles
Lowest Point: The Dead Sea (lowest point on Earth: 1,312 feet below sea level)
Population: 5,433,134
Form of Government: Republic
Chief crops: citrus and other fruit, vegetables, cotton, beef, dairy products
Major industries: machinery and equipment, cut diamonds, chemicals, textiles and apparel, metals, food processing
Natural resources: copper, sand, sulfur, asphalt, phosphates, clay
Basic Unit of Money: New Shekel
Main Languages: Hebrew (official), Arabic (used officially for Arab minority), English (most commonly used foreign language)
Major Religions: Judaism, Islam, Christianity

9% rural
91% urban
Population Distribution

Geography Skill Builder

Look at the map of Israel. Why do you think Israel has been called a "land bridge?"

Fishing in the Sea of Galilee

Israel is north of the **equator**. That means Israel is in the **Northern Hemisphere**. Israel is shaped like an arrow. Its tip points south. If you look at the map, you will also see that several areas of Israel are shaded orange. These orange territories are in dispute, or disagreement. Israel's neighbors —Egypt, Syria, Lebanon, and Jordan— have gone to war with Israel over who the land belongs to. They have been fighting for more than 50 years. They still don't all agree.

Israel is a tiny country. It is a bit bigger than the state of New Jersey. More than 5 million people live in Israel. That is less than the number of people who live in New York City.

For a tiny country, Israel has a big variety of landscapes. The waters along the western coast are called the Mediterranean Sea. This region forms the coastal **plain**. Here, there are warm temperatures and **fertile** soil. There is also water from two of Israel's major rivers, the Kishon and Yarkon. This land produces the **citrus** fruits that are most important to the country's farmers.

Industries on the western coast make many products, including **chemicals**, clothing, electronics, and polished diamonds. Because of the beautiful **climate**, fertile land, and many opportunities for work, this is the most densely populated part of the country.

Much of Israel is desert.

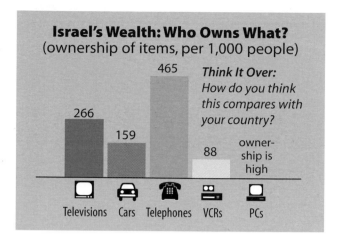

Israel's Wealth: Who Owns What?
(ownership of items, per 1,000 people)

Think It Over:
How do you think this compares with your country?

ownership is high

Televisions	Cars	Telephones	VCRs	PCs
266	159	465	88	

In the south is the Negev Desert. It takes up more than half of Israel's total land area. Because so much of the country is desert, water resources have always been a problem for Israel.

Along the entire eastern edge of the country is the Great Syrian-African Rift Valley. This is a deep, million-year-old split in the earth's crust. Here is the Jordan River—the country's largest river. The salty Dead Sea—the lowest place on Earth—is also located here.

The Many Communities of Israel

Israel is a mix of different peoples and ways of life. Whether they are Jews or Arabs, the people of Israel belong to many different communities.

Ethnic Communities

There are two major Jewish **ethnic groups** in Israel. One group is called the Ashkenazim. They are Jews who originally came from countries in northern and eastern Europe such as Germany, Russia, and Poland. The second group is called the Sephardim. They are Jews who originally came from Spain, Iran, Yemen, and Northern Africa. About half of the Jewish people in Israel were born outside the country. All together, they come from more than 70 different countries! All these different people also speak many different languages. But special classes run by the government have taught them to speak to one another in the same language—Hebrew.

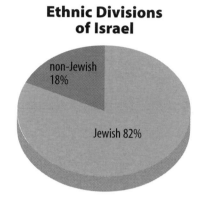

Ethnic Divisions of Israel

non-Jewish 18%

Jewish 82%

The third major ethnic group in Israel is made up of Arabic-speaking peoples. Two Arab groups play an important role in Israel's culture. They are the Bedouin and the Druze. Some Bedouin tribes are **nomadic**. That means they move from place to place. Bedouins pitch

A boy reads from the Torah as part of a bar-mitzvah ceremony.

their tents where they find food and water for their herds of sheep and goats. The Druze are mostly farmers. They have their own special religion, which they keep secret from outsiders.

Religious Communities

Israel was founded as a Jewish homeland. About 82% of the country's population is Jewish. Judaism is the world's oldest major religion. It is also the first to teach the belief in one God. Judaism's sacred book is called the Torah. It is made up of the first five books of the Bible. The Torah teaches Jewish history and the basic laws of Judaism. Jewish laws are

mostly concerned with teaching people to be good human beings and making the world a better place.

Most of Israel's Jews just observe the holidays and ceremonies of Jewish life. Two ceremonies are very important in a Jewish family. Baby boys are welcomed into the Jewish community with a naming ceremony called a brit. Part of this ceremony is a cutting of the foreskin (circumcision). At age 13, a boy is called to read from the Torah for the first time. This ceremony is

Major Religions of Israel

Christian 2%   Other 2%
Islam 14%
Judaism 82%

At a Glance

Holidays and Festivals

Because Israel is a Jewish state all Jewish holidays and festivals are national holidays.

Rosh Hashanah: Jewish New Year celebration that comes in the fall.

Yom Kippur: Jewish Day of Atonement (asking for forgiveness of sins). Comes eight days after Rosh Hashanah. Most holy day of the year.

Hanukkah: Eight day "Festival of Lights," usually comes in December. Celebrates the miracle of the "oil that burned for eight days" and the victory of a small group of Jewish soldiers. Candles are lighted, gifts are exchanged, games are played, and traditional foods are eaten.

Purim: Springtime festival that celebrates the story of Queen Esther saving the Jewish people from the wicked Hamen. Parades, costumes,

Brainstorm

Several of Israel's holidays are celebrated by eating special foods. Are there any holidays that you celebrate with special foods?

and triangular cookies filled with poppy seeds called "hamantaschen" are part of the merry-making.

Passover: Springtime Jewish freedom festival. Celebrates the escape of the Jewish people from slavery in Egypt. A family meal called a seder is served. Special foods without leavening (yeast) like matzo—a cracker-like bread— are eaten.

Day of Remembrance: Comes in the Spring. Honors those that gave their lives for Israel's independence.

Independence Day: The day after the Day of Remembrance. Celebrates the establishment of the State of Israel (1948) with parades, fireworks, and concerts.

★**Other Holidays**

Ramadan: A month long period of prayer and fasting observed by Muslims.

Celebrating with the traditional Passover seder.

44

The Al Aksa Mosque and the Golden Dome of the Rock can be seen above the Western Wall.

bar-mitzvah, which means "son of the commandments." This occasion marks the change from boyhood to manhood. Ceremonies for girls, called bat-mitzvahs, are less common.

Most of the rest of the people in Israel—about 14%—are **Muslims**. Muslims are followers of **Islam**. They read from their holy book called the Koran and pray to Allah. Their house of worship is called a **mosque**. Strict Muslims pray five times a day. Islam was founded by Muhammad. He is believed to be Allah's prophet, or messenger. Muslims also observe rituals of birth and manhood. Like Judaism, the traditional Muslim birth ceremony for boys also includes the rite of circumcision.

Only a small percentage of the population of Israel is Christian. But Israel is very important to Christians everywhere. Christians from all over the world travel to Israel each year to see where Jesus Christ lived, taught, and died.

Artistic and Cultural Communities

Arts and crafts are everywhere in Israel. There are huge sculptures in museums and parks. Colorful tile **mosaics** (decorations) cover the most important Muslim mosque near the Dome of the Rock. Glowing stained-glass windows can be seen in **synagogues** and churches. There are paintings, photographs, and pottery everywhere. And, because Israel is the holy land to Jews, Muslims, and Christians there are many beautiful religious objects.

Music is an important part of Israel's culture. Israelis enjoy listening to everything from folk songs to rock and roll. Going to concerts is a favorite activity.

Dance is popular, too. People get together for folk dancing at community centers. Street dancing is often part of holiday celebrations.

Israel is a nation of readers. Israelis read and publish more books per person than almost anywhere else in the world.

Daily Life

Daily life is different for the people of Israel depending on where they live. About 90% of the population lives in **urban** (city) areas. Most of these people make a living in business, industry, and the building trades. A small number of

Israelis are farmers. No matter where they live, people are part of many communities.

Educational Communities

Jews have been nicknamed "the People of the Book." Education is very important in Israel. Like in the United States, most Israeli children go to pre-school. But kids in Israel go to school six days a week! They have Friday, Saturday, or Sunday off—depending on whether they are Jewish, Muslim, or Christian. Most children of different religions go to different schools. They learn most of the same subjects that you do, such as math, science, and reading. Jewish kids also study the Bible and Jewish history. By fifth grade, all children study English. Arab children study the same basic subjects, but they learn about their own history, culture, and religion. After high school, most Jewish boys and girls are required to serve in the Israeli army.

Communities of Friends

Like you, kids in Israel enjoy being with friends. Playing sports, especially soccer, is one way friends spend time together. Another very popular activity is scouting. Almost every Israeli kid belongs to a youth group. Groups put together hiking, camping, and community service programs such as helping in a hospital. Community centers also sponsor after-school programs, where kids gather to do things like arts and craft projects.

Israel is filled with ancient ruins.

Community Project

Making Mosaic Tiles

Fancy tiles decorate the walls, floors, walls, and ceilings of many mosques in Israel. Since Muslim artists are forbidden by the Koran to show human or animal forms, the tile designs are usually complex patterns of shapes, flowers, or Arabic writing.

Materials

- Markers in two or three different colors
- 6" square pieces of white construction paper

Directions

- Look at the tile designs shown in the photo.
- Draw a pattern. Use the designs shown here or other combinations of shapes and flowers.
- Work with your classmates to mount your tiles on a bulletin board covered with blue paper. Blue is considered a lucky color in Muslim tradition. Place your tiles close together so that your display will look like a large mosaic wall.

Family Communities

Israeli families are very busy six days a week. In many families, both parents work. This means family time is very important. Friday evenings and Saturdays are special times for Jews because it is the Sabbath (day of rest). Buses don't run. Stores and businesses are closed. Most families enjoy a festive meal together that includes lighting candles. Some families attend religious services. Other families relax or visit friends. During holidays and school vacations, Israeli families enjoy exploring their country. Many go camping, have picnics, and hike to the country's many **ancient** ruins.

Jerusalem

Jerusalem is Israel's capital city. Because it is a holy city to three religions—Judaism, Islam, and Christianity—it has been fought over many times. This is especially sad because the city's name means "city of peace"

Jerusalem is like two cities in one. The eastern part of the city is called The Old City. The Old City is surrounded

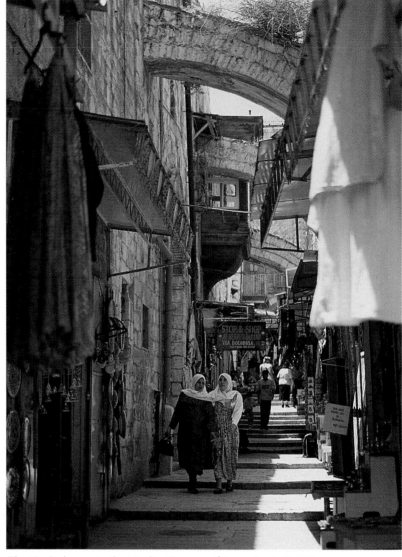

The Via Dolorosa in the Muslim Quarter of Jerusalem's Old City.

by 450-year-old stone walls. It is divided into four quarters—Jewish, Muslim, Christian, and Armenian. In the area called the Temple Mount is the Western or "Wailing" Wall. This is the holiest of Jewish sites. Near the Western Wall is the glittering Dome of the Rock, one of the holiest sites to Muslims. The Old City is alive with activity from morning to night. Visitors from all over the world shop in its open-air markets and peek into its ancient buildings. Alert young

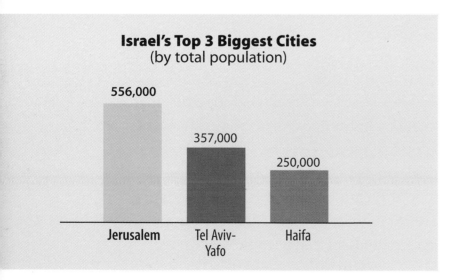

Israel's Top 3 Biggest Cities
(by total population)

556,000

357,000

250,000

Jerusalem | Tel Aviv-Yafo | Haifa

soldiers protect its winding streets. The New City is west of the Old City. Though some of the New City is quite old, most of it is modern. There are wonderful museums, fancy shops, tall

Brainstorm

1. Which part of Jerusalem would you rather visit, the Old City or the New City?

2. Many ruins in Jerusalem are more than 2,000 years old! What's the oldest thing in your city or town?

Geography Skill Builder

1. Can you find Jerusalem on the map?

2. Which cities do you think are part of the western coastal plain?

office buildings, and quiet neighbor-hoods. The Knesset is the government building where Israel's laws are made. It is located in the New City, too.

Girls from Jerusalem gather outside in one of the city's parks.

England

It's a long plane flight across the Atlantic Ocean to England. But when you land, you may find that you don't feel like you've left home at all! This is not so surprising. A little more than 200 years ago, our country was an English **colony**. Our language and many of our laws have been borrowed from English **traditions**.

England is part of a European nation called The United Kingdom of Great Britain and Northern Ireland (UK). It is the largest country in the UK. England is part of the island of Great Britain. It lies northwest of the **continent** of Europe. Scotland and Wales are the other two countries that make up the island.

Map Key
★ Capital City
● Major City

EUROPE
Equator
SCOTLAND
NORTH SEA
NORTHERN IRELAND
ISLE OF MAN
IRISH SEA
IRELAND
N W E S
● Manchester
● Birmingham
WALES
NORTH ATLANTIC OCEAN
London
Thames River
NORTH ATLANTIC OCEAN
Strait of Dover
ENGLISH CHANNEL
FRANCE

At a Glance

Official Name: United Kingdom of Great Britain and Northern Ireland
Capital: London
Area (U.K.): 94,525 square miles
Population (U.K.): 58,295,119
Form of Government: Constitutional monarchy

10% rural
90% urban
Population Distribution

Chief crops: sugar beets, potatoes, wheat, barley, dairy products
Major industries: manufactured goods, machinery, fuels, transport equipment, food processing
Natural resources: coal, petroleum, natural gas, tin, limestone, iron ore, salt, clay, chalk, gypsum, lead
Basic Unit of Money: Pound
Main Languages (U.K.): English, Welsh (about 26% of the population of Wales), Scottish form of Gaelic (about 60,000 in Scotland)
Major Religions (U.K.): Anglicanism, Roman Catholicism, Islam, Presbyterianism, Methodism, Sikhism, Hinduism, Judaism

England is north of the **equator**. That means it is in the **Northern Hemisphere**. On its western coast are the Irish Sea and the North Atlantic Ocean. On its eastern coast is the North Sea. England is separated from France in the south by only 21 miles of the English Channel. In 1994, the Channel Tunnel (nicknamed "The Chunnel") connected England and

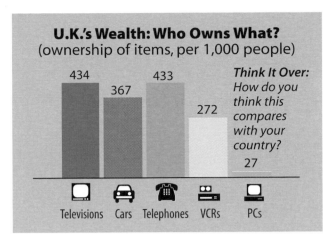

U.K.'s Wealth: Who Owns What?
(ownership of items, per 1,000 people)

Televisions	Cars	Telephones	VCRs	PCs
434	367	433	272	27

Think It Over: How do you think this compares with your country?

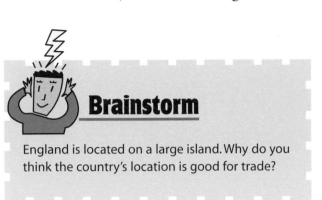

Brainstorm

England is located on a large island. Why do you think the country's location is good for trade?

France. Now cars and trucks whisk passengers and freight between the two countries under the channel!

England is a small, crowded country. Its total land area is slightly over 50,000 square miles—that's roughly the size of the state of New York. About 48 million people live in England.

Rugged highlands are found in the north and southwestern areas of the country. In the center and southeast are low-lying **plains** and valleys. Most people live in these areas.

England's long coastline makes fishing an important **industry**.

Rolling green hills and valleys make the English countryside perfect for picnics.

The Many Communities of England

England's communities are an interesting mix of tradition and change.

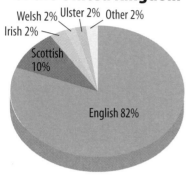

Ethnic Divisions of the United Kingdom

Welsh 2% Ulster 2% Other 2%
Irish 2%
Scottish 10%
English 82%

Ethnic Communities

There are three major **ethnic groups** in England. The largest group is **descended** from various European peoples. These were peoples that settled in the country over thousands of years.

The second-largest group is Asian, especially from Pakistan and India.

The third group is Afro-Caribbean. They are mostly from the West Indies.

Immigrant groups were asked to come to England because the country needed workers. Many faced **prejudice** in jobs, education, and housing.

England's schoolchildren reflect the country's ethnic mix.

Westminster Abbey is one of England's most famous churches.

Religious Communities

England is officially a Christian country, but it has religious freedom. The Church of England is also called the Anglican Church. It is England's official church. The **monarch** (king or queen) is its ceremonial head. It is a Protestant church, but services and religious practices vary. More than half of English people belong to the Church of England. About 20% attend church regularly.

Roman Catholics make up the second-largest religious group.

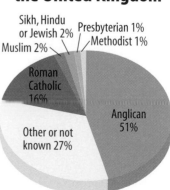

Major Religions of the United Kingdom

Sikh, Hindu or Jewish 2%   Presbyterian 1%
Muslim 2%   Methodist 1%
Roman Catholic 16%
Other or not known 27%
Anglican 51%

At a Glance

Holidays and Festivals

★National Holidays

The Trooping of Colours: Second Saturday in June. Celebrates the queen's official birthday. The queen inspects the troops that make up her personal guard.

Armistice Day: Sunday closest to November 11. Honors those who died in world wars. A procession is led by the queen. Wreaths are placed at a memorial.

★Christian Holidays

Christmas and Easter: Celebrated like in other westernized countries.

Maundy Thursday: The day before Good Friday. The queen gives out specially minted coins to poor men and women.

Christmas carolers at the London Bridge.

★Other Holidays

Guy Fawkes Night (Bonfire Night): November 5. Remembers the plot by Guy Fawkes to blow up Parliament almost 400 years ago. Celebrated with bonfires, pranks, fireworks, and the burning of straw dummies or "guys." Similar to American Halloween.

Brainstorm

Here are some everyday words used by kids in England. Can you figure out what they mean?
1. cooker 2. lift 3. bobby 4. sweet 5. lorry 6. sledge

Answers: 1. stove 2. elevator 3. police officer 4. candy 5. truck 6. sled

The largest group of non-Christian people are **Muslims**. Muslims follow the religion of **Islam**. Islam teaches a belief in one god, called Allah.

England has many people who practice religions such as Sikhism, Buddhism, and Hinduism. The country also has one of the largest Jewish populations in Europe.

Artistic and Cultural Communities

England is probably best known for its many famous writers. William Shakespeare wrote plays more than 400 years ago. They are still read and performed in countries around the world. Movies like *Romeo & Juliet* have been made of many of his plays, too. Lewis Carroll, the author of *Alice in Wonderland*, was English. So was Beatrix Potter who wrote *The Tale of Peter Rabbit*. Charles Dickens wrote the famous holiday story, *A Christmas Carol*.

William Shakespeare

53

In the 1960's rock and roll music was changed forever by an English group called The Beatles. They had many hit records. The Rolling Stones, Eric Clapton, and Elton John are other famous English music superstars.

Daily Life

Life in England is similar to life in other western countries. More than 90% of English people live in **urban** (city) areas. Most citizens work in jobs that provide services for other people. These services include banking, health care, and **transportation**. They also include education, tourism, and shopkeeping. Many other people work in manufacturing jobs. In the countryside, there are many modern cattle and sheep farms.

Educational Communities

If you visited an English classroom, you would probably feel right at home.

Like you, children speak English. That is England's official language. But their

Students from Lincolnshire do an experiment in chemistry class.

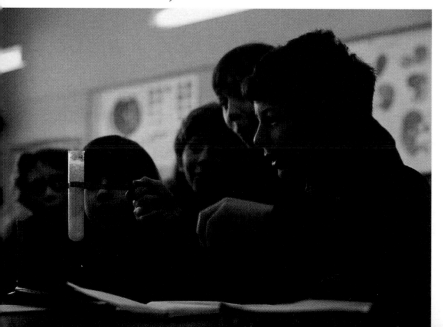

Word Watch

One of the most popular sports in England is football. But it's not football the way you think of it. In England, football is what Americans call soccer! What's like American football? It's the game called rugby.

English is not exactly the same as yours. If you spoke to some kids, you would realize that certain words are different. For example, they would say "ta" for "thank-you" and "ring me up" instead of "call me on the phone."

All children between the ages of 5 and 16 must attend school. About 90% of children go to free state schools. This is paid for by the government. Boarding schools are common in England as well. Starting in elementary, students live at school instead of home. They live in group settings called **dormitories**. Most American boarding schools were created from the English model.

Communities of Friends

Popular English outdoor activities are skating, bicycle riding, or going to a park. Indoors, playing board games or computer games is popular. Snooker, a game like pool, is also fun.

There are thousands of sports clubs across the country. Most English kids participate in at least one organized team sport. Soccer is the most popular. Friends enjoy playing, going to watch their favorite teams compete, and trading

Community Project

Make a Coat of Arms

Long ago, English knights wore armor to protect themselves in battle. It was hard to tell a friend from an enemy under metal masks and suits. Knights began displaying emblems (pictures) on their shields, such as a tree or a lion. Then others could recognize them in battle.

Materials

- white construction paper
- colorful markers

Directions

- Look at the coats of arms.
- Draw a large shield shape in the center of your paper.
- Decide on figure such as an animal, plant, castle, sword, or other object you would like to represent you. Draw it in the center of your shield.
- Add decorations such as geometric shapes or designs.
- Think of a **motto** or saying that represents your personality. Write it in fancy letters.

soccer cards (like baseball cards). Cricket is like baseball. It is played with a flat bat and a ball. It is very popular, too. It has been called England's national sport.

Rugby is a popular sport in England.

Family Communities

Most families in England are small. There are usually two adults and one or two children. Almost half of women work. The majority of English families own their own small homes. Land is **scarce** so many houses in towns are attached to one another. Gardening in small gardens is a popular hobby.

Pets are important family members. About half of all English families have pets. Dogs are the favorite choice.

Sunday lunch is a family **tradition**. Eating out is a special treat. Fish and chips (french fries) is the favorite English "fast-food."

London

London is the capital of the entire United Kingdom. It is one of the world's largest and greatest cities. London is a fascinating mixture of old and new. About 7 million people live there. Millions of tourists visit each year.

London is a **port** city. That has helped to make it a center for business. England depends on world trade. Banks, insurance companies, and shipping firms do business with countries around the world. The London Stock Exchange is one of the world's top business centers.

Like most English cities, London is also an important manufacturing center. Factories in and around London produce

London's clock tower is named Big Ben. It is one of the city's most famous landmarks.

Geography Skill Builder

Find London on the map of England. Why do you think the city became England's most important business center? Why do you think London is located where it is on the island?

clothing, food products, and tools. They also produce household appliances, cars, pottery, and printed materials like books and newspapers.

The country's major government buildings are located in London. The Houses of Parliament (where laws are made) are there. So is Buckingham Palace. That's the official home of the royal family. London's Westminster Abbey is the most famous of England's churches. Kings and queens have been crowned there for **centuries**. England's royal family no longer rules the nation. Instead it is ruled by a prime minister, a group of government officials (called the Cabinet), and a Parliament (like a congress).

History is everywhere in London. St. Paul's Cathedral is almost 300 years old. That is where the famous wedding of Prince Charles and Lady Diana took place. The well-known Tower of London is a palace that was turned into a prison. It is the city's oldest landmark—nearly 1,000 years old!

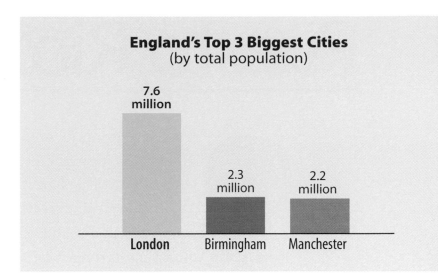

England's Top 3 Biggest Cities
(by total population)

City	Population
London	7.6 million
Birmingham	2.3 million
Manchester	2.2 million

London also has colorful markets, fashionable shops, and many theaters. Going to the theater is one of London's most popular nights out.

A troupe of guards marches in front of London's Buckingham Palace.

Puerto Rico

If you live in the United States, Puerto Rico is closer than you may think. It is located only 1,000 miles southeast of the state of Florida. And, if you visit there, you won't really have left the United States at all! Puerto Rico is a U.S. **commonwealth**. That means it receives certain protections and services from the U.S. government. Puerto Ricans are American **citizens**. They can live, work, and travel freely in the United States. Puerto Ricans who live on the island, however, may not vote in presidential elections.

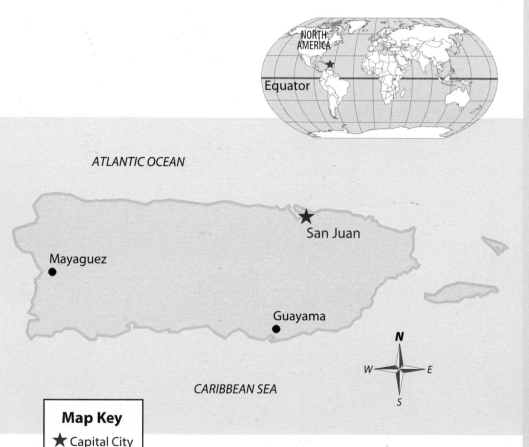

ATLANTIC OCEAN

★ San Juan

Mayaguez

Guayama

CARIBBEAN SEA

Map Key
★ Capital City
● Major City

At a Glance

Official Name: Commonwealth of Puerto Rico
Capital: San Juan
Area: 3,508 square miles
Population: 3,812,569
Form of Government: Commonwealth associated with the United States
Chief crops: coffee, plaintains, pineapples, sugarcane, bananas
Major industries: pharmaceuticals, electronics, apparel, food products, instruments, tourism
Natural resources: some copper and nickel, potential for onshore and offshore crude oil
Basic Unit of Money: U.S. dollar
Main Languages: Spanish, English
Major Religions: Roman Catholicism, Protestantism

33% rural / 67% urban

Population Distribution

Puerto Rico is a small rectangular-shaped island. It is slightly smaller than the state of Connecticut. More than 3.5 million people live there.

Puerto Rico is north of the **equator**. That means it is in the **Northern Hemisphere**. It belongs to an **archipelago**, or group of islands. This group is known as the West Indies or Antilles. North of the island is the Atlantic Ocean. South of the island is the Caribbean Sea. To the west is Puerto Rico's closest neighbor,

Geography Skill Builder

Puerto Rico means "rich port" in Spanish. It was originally the name of the city of San Juan. Over the years, the whole island became known as Puerto Rico. Why do you think this might be a good name?

the Dominican Republic. To the east are the Virgin Islands, which are also part of the West Indies.

Tiny Puerto Rico has a variety of physical features. Three quarters of it is mountainous. Its mountains in the northeast make up the only tropical rainforest in the United States! Along the coastal areas stretch beautiful sandy beaches. They draw millions of visitors each year. Tourism is a very important **industry** on the island. The northern coast is the popular vacation spot for most travelers. It is also the island's most heavily populated area. Here are the many high-rise hotels, resorts, and apartment buildings.

Puerto Rico is an island that is protected by the United States.

The Many Communities of Puerto Rico

Puerto Ricans belong to many different communities. And, because the island is a U.S. commonwealth, there is also a large community of Puerto Ricans who live on the U.S mainland. Most make their homes in New York City.

Ethnic Divisions of Puerto Rico

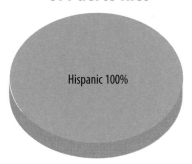

Hispanic 100%

Ethnic Communities

Puerto Rico is a mix of different Hispanic **ethnic groups**. Christopher Columbus claimed the island for Spain in 1493. Spain controlled Puerto Rico for more than 400 years. Many Spanish settlers married the peaceful native people, called the Taino. Others married African slaves who had been brought to work on the island's sugar plantations. As a result, most of Puerto Rico's people are of Spanish **descent**. Spanish and English are the island's official languages.

In the last 200 years, people have come to Puerto Rico from China, Lebanon, Venezuela, Europe, and the United States. The island has also been a safe place for people fleeing problems in other islands in the West Indies.

Religious Communities

Religion is very important in Puerto Rico. For example, when a new business or office opens, priests bless the event.

Almost all of the people of Puerto Rico are Christian. About 15% of the population practices several Protestant faiths. But, the most common religion in Puerto Rico is Catholicism. Catholicism was brought to Puerto Rico by Spanish settlers more than 300 years ago. Today, about 85% of Puerto Ricans are Roman Catholic. But their practices are often a

Most of Puerto Rico's people are of Spanish descent.

blend of Catholic beliefs and Indian and African beliefs. Most families have pictures or wooden statues of saints, called santos, in their homes. People often ask their santos for help or protection. Children are usually **baptized** by a priest soon after they are born. At age 7, they make their first Holy Communion. When they are between 11 and 13, they are usually confirmed in the church. At that time they take another name. Usually, it is the name of their favorite saint.

The influence of Indian and African spiritualism can be seen throughout the country. Spiritualists are people who are believed to have special powers. Some believe they can contact the dead, heal the sick, or tell the future. Some traditional spiritual ceremonies and customs are still observed, especially in **rural** areas. For example, a whole village may join in prayer for rain. People may also carry charms to keep evil away.

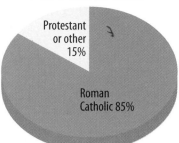

Major Religions of Puerto Rico

Protestant or other 15%

Roman Catholic 85%

At a Glance

Holidays and Festivals

The people of Puerto Rico celebrate most major American holidays. They also celebrate many days that honor important leaders and mark events in the island's history.

★Religious Holidays

Las Navidades (Christmas): December 25. Celebrated with church attendance, a feast with special foods, gift giving, and surprise visits to friends.

Three Kings' Day: January 6. Children receive gifts in exchange for the small boxes of grass they have left for the horses of the three Wise Men.

Feast of San Juan Bautista: June 23. Celebrated with a picnic at the beach and a re-creation of the baptism of Jesus Christ. Honors St. John the Baptist, the island's patron saint.

A young girl is dressed for the annual carnival in San Juan.

Feast of Santiago Apostol: July 25. Celebrated with a parade of masked and costumed dancers. Honors St. James the Apostle.

★Other Festivals

Pablo Casals Festival: Spring. Established by the famous cellist, whose mother was Puerto Rican. Celebrates classical music.

61

Artistic and Cultural Communities

Puerto Rico is probably best known for its important contributions to the world of music. Traditional Puerto Rican music has Taino, Spanish, and African roots. The influence of African rhythms is heard in the popular style of music called salsa. The word means "sauce" and it refers to salsa's "spicy" hot sound. Tito Puente, a Puerto Rican American, made salsa music popular in the United States. Classical music in Puerto Rico was established by the famous cellist, Pablo Casals. He started a music school, a symphony orchestra, and a yearly music festival.

Daily Life

Daily life in Puerto Rico has changed over the last 40 years. Most people used to live and work in farming villages. Now, about two thirds of the people live in cities and urban areas.

Brainstorm

Climate affects peoples lives. It influences the clothing they wear, the food they eat, the houses they live in and the activities they enjoy. What is the climate like where you live? How does it affect *how* you live?

Educational Communities

Puerto Rico became a U.S. territory more than 100 years ago. Back then, only one out of four people could read. Today, more than 90% of the population can read and write. The Puerto Rican school system is very similar to yours. But, students learn their lessons in Spanish. English is taught as a second language in all schools.

Communities of Friends

Basketball is Puerto Rico's most popular sport. In San Juan, kids have fun at a

A vendor displays some traditional Puerto Rican fried foods.

Community Project

Making Masks

Mask making is a folk art form in Puerto Rico. Special *veigante* masks are carved from coconuts or wood. They are worn at the popular Feast of Santiago Apostol. Masks shaped like animal heads are also carved.

Materials
- sturdy paper plates
- markers or paint
- feathers, yarn, buttons, beads, crepe-paper streamers
- craft sticks or elastic
- scissors, tape, staplers, glue

Directions
- Find a drawing or a picture of an animal you want to represent.
- Use markers or paint to color your plate.
- Add features with buttons, beads, or yarn.
- Use feathers and streamers to decorate your mask.
- When your mask is done and dry, tape a craft stick to the back of the plate to use as a handle.

"sports city" dedicated to Roberto Clemente. He is the island's most famous baseball hero. And, because Puerto Rico is an island, the beach is always close by. Water sports such as swimming and surfing are popular activities.

One of the activities friends enjoy most is going to festivals. Each town organizes one to honor its patron saint. There is usually a fairground with rides, parades, and pageants. Food, music, and dancing are also part of the fun.

Family Communities

Most modern families in Puerto Rico are similar to families in the United States. But, one important Puerto Rican family custom is less common in America. That is the practice of a child having a *compadre* (godfather) or *comadre* (godmother). This is a very close and special family relationship. If necessary, the godparent may even raise the child.

Students work together at San Juan University.

San Juan

San Juan is Puerto Rico's capital city. It is also its center of business and culture. More than 1 million people live there. That's a third of the island's population. Millions of tourists visit San Juan every year.

High-rises and hotels line San Juan's sandy beaches.

San Juan is really two cities in one. Old San Juan is located on an island. It is connected to the main island by several bridges and a highway. Here, narrow, winding streets lead to quiet plazas. Ancient church **steeples** and massive **forts** have been preserved. Many were built by the Spanish hundreds of years ago. The most famous reminder of the Spanish is the huge fort on San Juan bay called

Brainstorm

Tourists visiting San Juan can visit beaches, forts, theatres, and shops. They can attend festivals and hear a symphony orchestra. What are some things a tourist visiting your city or state can do?

El Morro. It is one of Puerto Rico's most-recognized lanmarks.

The Condado district is the business center of San Juan. It is very different from the historic feeling of old San Juan. Here, high-rise hotels stretch along busy beaches. Modern office buildings and elegant stores crowd the landscape. Tourists and buses fill the busy streets. San Juan is also one of the busiest **ports** in the West Indies.

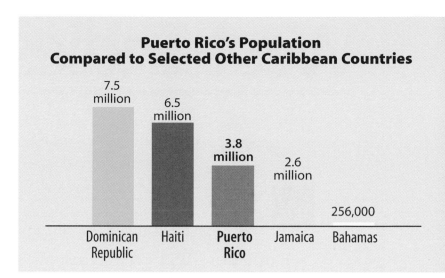

**Puerto Rico's Population
Compared to Selected Other Caribbean Countries**

Dominican Republic	Haiti	Puerto Rico	Jamaica	Bahamas
7.5 million	6.5 million	3.8 million	2.6 million	256,000

An ancient wall surrounds Old San Juan.

West Indies

From the name you might think that the West Indies are located near India. So did Christopher Columbus. Columbus was the first European to reach the islands. He named them the Indies because he thought he had sailed to India! Later, the islands were given the name West Indies. That's so people wouldn't confuse them with the East Indies islands off the coast of Asia.

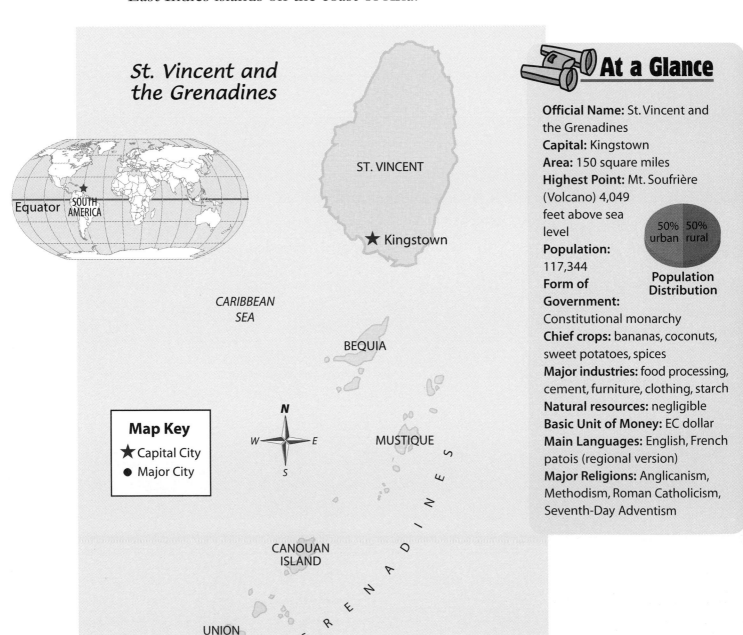

St. Vincent and the Grenadines

Equator

SOUTH AMERICA

ST. VINCENT

★ Kingstown

CARIBBEAN SEA

BEQUIA

Map Key
★ Capital City
● Major City

N
W E
S

MUSTIQUE

CANOUAN ISLAND

UNION ISLAND

GRENADINES

At a Glance

Official Name: St. Vincent and the Grenadines
Capital: Kingstown
Area: 150 square miles
Highest Point: Mt. Soufrière (Volcano) 4,049 feet above sea level
Population: 117,344
Form of Government: Constitutional monarchy
Chief crops: bananas, coconuts, sweet potatoes, spices
Major industries: food processing, cement, furniture, clothing, starch
Natural resources: negligible
Basic Unit of Money: EC dollar
Main Languages: English, French patois (regional version)
Major Religions: Anglicanism, Methodism, Roman Catholicism, Seventh-Day Adventism

50% urban 50% rural

Population Distribution

The West Indies are located north of the **equator**. That means they are in the **Northern Hemisphere**. The islands are in a **tropical** (warm) area just north of the equator. That means they have a warm, moist climate that is good for growing things. Most people in the West Indies make their living as farmers. Sugar cane, bananas and other fruits, coffee, cotton, and tobacco are important crops.

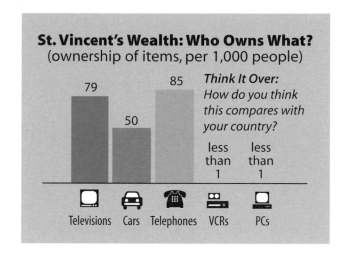

St. Vincent's Wealth: Who Owns What?
(ownership of items, per 1,000 people)

Think It Over: How do you think this compares with your country?

Televisions	Cars	Telephones	VCRs	PCs
79	50	85	less than 1	less than 1

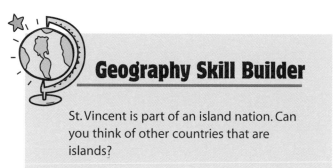

Geography Skill Builder

St. Vincent is part of an island nation. Can you think of other countries that are islands?

The West Indies are an **archipelago**, or island chain. The chain is made up of thousands of islands. They stretch for more than 2,000 miles in the Caribbean Sea between North and South America. Most of the islands are the tops of undersea mountains. Many were formed by volcanoes. Some are still active. Others are made of coral.

Bright sandy beaches, clear blue waters, and mild temperatures attract millions of visitors from all over the world. Tourism is very important to the islands. Fine harbors and deep bays provide welcoming **ports** for both cruise ships and trade.

Coconut palms fill the island of St. Vincent.

The islands are very beautiful, but their peaceful settings are sometimes disturbed by violent hurricanes. Heavy rains and powerful hurricane winds destroy buildings, homes, factories, and crops.

The Many Communities of the West Indies

About 35 million people live on the 24 inhabited islands of the West Indies. Each island is a community. But the islands have a similar history and share many characteristics.

Ethnic Communities

Most of the people who live in the West Indies are of African descent. Africans were brought by the French, Spanish, English, and Dutch who used slaves on sugar plantations. The rest of the people are mostly of mixed black African and European **ancestry**.

West Indians speak different languages. Which language depends on which country has controlled their island. Spanish, French, Dutch, and English are common official languages. Many West Indians speak Creole languages.

These are a combination of African languages and either Spanish or French.

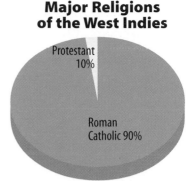

Major Religions of the West Indies

Protestant 10%

Roman Catholic 90%

Though the islands are a mixture of races, there is **prejudice** against darker skinned peoples. White West Indians and lighter-skinned peoples mostly have the best jobs and more comfortable lifestyles.

Religious Communities

Most West Indians are Christian. Catholicism was brought by Spanish and French settlers. It is the most common religion. Several Protestant faiths are practiced on the islands that were settled by the English and the Dutch.

Many people practice a blend of traditional African religions and Christianity. On Jamaica, Pocomania has

Islanders perform a baptism in a river.

many followers. Through their rituals, believers hope that they will be possessed by spirits. Afterwards, these spirits will be their protectors. Voodoo is so strong on Haiti that it is recognized as an official religion. There are Voodoo gods of fire, war, love, water, and other things. Drum music, singing, and dancing are important parts of the ceremonies of many traditional island religions. Believers often go into **trance**-like states.

Rastafarianism began on the island of Jamaica. It is based on several of the books of the Bible. Its name comes from Ras Tafari, a title of the last emperor of Ethiopia, a country in Africa. Many Rastafarians believe that Africa is the true home of people of African **descent**. Rastafarians try to eat only natural food. They do not eat pork or drink milk, coffee, or alcohol. Most wear their hair in "dreadlocks" (tight rope-like braids). The famous reggae (RE•gay) style of music comes from Rastafarian roots.

Artistic and Cultural Communities

The West Indies are best known for their strong traditions in music and dance. Different religions and peoples have each added their influences to the islands' sound. Drums, guitars, flute-like

---

 **At a Glance**

Holidays and Festivals

★**National Holidays**

Independence Days: Celebrated at various times on islands that are independent nations. Parades, contests, musical and artistic events, even gift-giving are part of the festivities on different islands.

★**Other Holidays**

Carnival: Celebrated on many of the islands. Festivities last several days in late winter or early spring. They include parades with marchers in elaborate costumes and fantastic masks, music, dancing, and special foods.

Christmas and Easter: Mostly religious holidays. Christmas trees are rare.

Gift-giving is simple. Special meals are enjoyed with family and friends.

Diwali: Fall. Hindu New Year celebration. Celebrated by West Indians of East Indian descent.

Ramadan: Winter. Month of fasting celebrated by Muslim West Indians.

 **Brainstorm**

Music and dancing play an important part in festivals in the West Indies. Do you celebrate any holidays with music, dancing, or singing? Why do you think music is an important part of the celebrations of so many cultures?

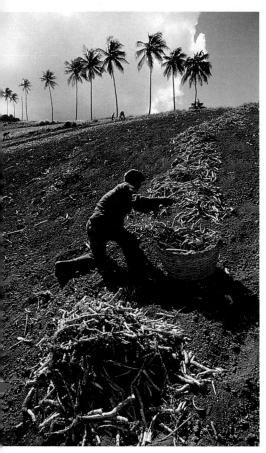

A farmer works harvesting arrowroot.

instruments, and instruments such as maracas (rattles) and claves (sticks) are important elements in most island music.

Reggae music from Jamaica has become popular all over the world. Its lyrics describe everyday problems. They often have important Rastafarian religious messages about peace and love. Jamaican musician Bob Marley was a reggae superstar.

Calypso music from Trinidad is a blend of Asian, Spanish, and African influences. Steel drums, or "pans," made from recycled oil drums add a special sound to this music.

Salsa music from Puerto Rico and Cuba is fast, hot, and "spicy" like its name, which means "sauce."

Exciting dances like the mambo, rumba, cha-cha, and the merengue all come from the islands. You may have done the West Indian dance called the limbo at a party.

Daily Life

How people live depends on which island is their home. Each island has different customs and communities.

Educational Communities

Schools on the islands of the West Indies are free for students between the ages of 5 and 16. Most schools are located in towns and cities. Children who live in **rural** areas must often walk long distances to get to school each day. Going to school in shifts is common because there are not enough classrooms for everyone. Wealthy families often send their children to private schools run by churches.

Most West Indian children wear uniforms to school. Classes are taught in the official language of the island— Spanish, French, Dutch, or English. Children usually also learn English if it is not their native language.

Because many of the islands are poor, children often drop out to get jobs to help their families. This commonly happens when a child reaches the age of 12 or 13. On Haiti, the poorest of the islands, only one child in ten finishes elementary school.

Communities of Friends

Because of the mild weather, kids can enjoy the beautiful sandy beaches and warm blue water nearly all year round. Swimming, surfing, and snorkeling are popular island activities.

Away from the beaches, friends play games like chess, checkers, and dominoes. Sports are also popular. Islanders like to watch baseball, soccer, and cricket teams, or play those games themselves. Volleyball or "net ball" is another favorite.

Community Project

Making Murals

Bright, colorful murals decorate churches, airports, public buildings, and slum walls all over the West Indies. Their subjects are drawn from life on the islands.

Materials

- paints
- brushes
- a large piece of white paper

Directions

- Chose an interesting part of island culture such as family life, sports, festivals, music and dance, food, land, plants and animals. Or chose a specific island to learn about.
- Find out more about your topic from books, encyclopedias, or web sites.
- Paint a scene based on the facts you learned.
- OPTIONAL: Put your scene together with your classmates to create a large mural for a wall in your classroom.

Because many of the people in the West Indies are poor, kids in the countryside often have jobs to do. Many must care for younger siblings. Some cook and clean. Others help their parents in the fields. In the cities, children as young as 7 or 8 may work selling newspapers or even shining shoes.

Family Communities

The extended family is especially important in the West Indies. It is made up of grandparents, cousins, and relatives who live close by. **Poverty** often forces men to move around looking for jobs. Some even have to move to other countries. As a result, women are the heads of many West Indian families.

Some white families still practice European customs, such as formal tea on the lawn.

St. Vincent

Saint Vincent and the Grenadines is a young country. It has only been independent since 1979. Before that, it was ruled by Great Britain for almost 200 years.

The entire country is made up of the island of St. Vincent and about 100 smaller islands. The smaller islands lie in a chain called the Grenadines. Tropical plants covers most of the mountainous island. An active volcano, Mt. Soufrière, erupted during the nation's first year of independence!

As in most of the West Indies, the majority of the country's more than 100,000 people are descendants of black African slaves.

Most people live in rural areas and work on farms. Important crops are

The St. Vincent town of Fancy was covered in ash after the Mt. Soufrière volcano erupted in 1979.

bananas, coconuts, spices, and arrowroot—a starch used in baby food.

One of the worst problems on the islands is a lack of jobs. To ease this problem, the government has been trying to grow its tourist **industry**. Airports and runways are being redone. New hotels are being built. In recent years, islands like St. Vincent, St. Lucia, and St. Kitts have seen growth in tourism. Warm climates, clean and sandy beaches, and a friendly atmosphere attract many visitors. Much has been done to improve the area around the beautiful harbor in St. Vincent's capital, Kingstown.

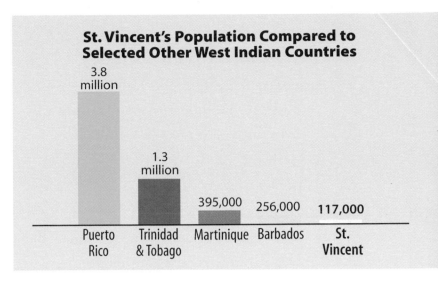

St. Vincent's Population Compared to Selected Other West Indian Countries

Puerto Rico	Trinidad & Tobago	Martinique	Barbados	St. Vincent
3.8 million	1.3 million	395,000	256,000	117,000

Islanders in Kingstown play dominoes to pass the time.

Student Glossary

ancestry Family and ethnic background; descent. Members of your family who lived long ago are your ancestors.

apartheid South Africa's government policy of separating citizens by race.

archipelago An island chain made up of many islands nearby one another. The West Indies is an archipelago.

architecture Buildings and structures. High-rises, churches, and bridges make up the architecture of many cities.

atheist One who denies God's existence.

baptism Religious ceremony whereby Christian babies are ritually bathed as a welcome into the religious community.

calligraphy The art of fine writing. Wedding invitations often have beautiful calligraphy.

century Time period consisting of 100 years. 400 years is four centuries.

chemical A substance, usually human-made, designed to perform a specific function.

citizens People who are granted full rights under the government of a country. U.S. citizens can vote, get U.S. passports, and are protected by the Constitution.

citrus Kind of fruit that typically has thick rind, pulpy flesh, and high acid content.

climate Common weather; atmospheric conditions. The climate of most Caribbean islands is warm.

colony A body of people living in a new land but keeping ties to an old country or state. English settlers first formed successful colonies in America in the 1600s.

commonwealth An association of self-governing states or nations that share a common leadership or crown. Puerto Rico is a commonwealth that is protected by the United States.

Communist/communism A form of government in which a single party has total authority over most aspects of daily life, including the country's economy.

compass A navigation tool that indicates direction (north, south, east, west).

continent A large, continuous mass of land. The seven continents of the world are Asia, Australia, Antarctica, North America, South America, Africa, and Europe.

democracy A government by the people, where citizens control the power. The United States of America is a democracy.

descendant/descent A person from a previous generation with whom blood or stock is hared; family line. You are a descendant of your ancestors.

dormitory Group housing complex; usually in a school or institutional environment.

equator An imaginary line around the exact middle of the earth that separates the Northern Hemisphere from the Southern Hemisphere.

ethnic group A group of people that share a common racial, national, tribal, religious, or cultural background.

fertile Rich, productive. Fertile soil produces plentiful crops.

fortress Walls and structures built for the purpose of protection.

graze To feed upon the growth of a pasture or meadow. Cows graze in their pastures.

heritage Something passed on by previous members of a family or cultural group. People who work to preserve their family history are proud of their heritage.

Hinduism An ancient Indian religion that has elements of mysticism.

Islam A religion based on the teachings of the prophet Muhammed, who taught others to worship a single god, Allah.

immigrant A person who comes to a new country to set up a life. The United States is a nation of immigrants from many countries.

industry Major business.

invent First create. Fireworks were invented in China.

metro Subway.

monarch King or queen.

mosaic Artistic design or image created with a series of many small pieces, commonly ceramic tile.

mosque Islamic house of worship.

Muslim A follower of the religion of Islam.

nomadic Moving from place to place; without a permanent home.

Northern Hemisphere The half of the Earth that is above (north of) the equator.

pastime Recreation; entertainment. Baseball has been called "America's national pastime."

patriotism Pride in country. Waving or saluting your country's flag shows patriotism.

plain A large area of flat or gently rolling treeless land.

plateau A large area of flat land that is raised high above the surrounding land.

port Harbor. Ships pull into port to load or unload their cargo.

poverty Poorness; extreme lack. People without proper clothing, food, or shelter live in poverty.

prejudice Prejudgment of someone based on a general characteristic, such as skin color, religion, or ethnic background. Minority groups in the United States have faced prejudice in the past.

porcelain A hard ceramic. Expensive teapots and collector's dolls are often made of fine porcelain.

prophet A person who has special powers of insight; usually spiritual. Muhammed was the prophet who brought the word of the god Allah to the people.

residence Home. The official residence of England's queen is Buckingham Palace in London. A resident is one who lives in a particular place.

rural Country-like; opposite of urban. Much of America's Midwest is rural farmland.

scarce In short supply. In the desert, water is scarce.

segregate Separate. The system of apartheid segregated South Africans based on the color of their skin.

shrine Structure or place to worship or adore a particular being.

slum A heavily populated, dirty, run-down living area. Many big cities around the world have slums, where people live in poverty.

Southern Hemisphere The half of the Earth that is below (south of) the equator.

steeple Tall structure, usually with a pointy roof, at the top of a church.

steppe A flat, treeless plain.

suburb An outlying part of a city or town; usually more residential, neighborhood-like.

synagogue Jewish house of worship.

tradition Custom; an established practice or style that has been used for a long period of time. For a couple's twenty-fifth wedding anniversary it is a tradition to give a gift of something silver.

trait A distinguishing quality. Honesty is a good character trait.

trance State of being hypnotized or deeply involved in something.

transportation Way of getting around.

tundra A flat, treeless, snow-covered plain. Cold, Arctic-like places like Siberia and Alaska are usually mostly tundra.

urban Heavily populated, city-like.

veld South African grassland.

For More Information

Further Reading

Blashfield, Jean F. *Enchantment of the World: England*. Danbury, CT: Children's Press, 1997.

Blauer, Ettagale. *Enchantment of the World: South Africa*. Danbury, CT: Children's Press, 1998.

Canesso, Claudia. *Places and Peoples of the World: South Africa*. New York: Chelsea House, 1989.

Charley, Catherine. *Country Fact Files: China*. Madison, NJ: Raintree/Steck-Vaughn, 1995.

Fradin, Judith Bloom. *From Sea to Shining Sea: Puerto Rico*. Chicago: Children's Press, 1995.

Ganeri, Anita. *Exploration into India*. New York: New Discovery, 1995.

Hodge, Alison Caribbean. *Country Fact Files: The West Indies*. Madison, NJ: Raintree/Steck-Vaughn, 1998.

Jones, Helen H. *Enchantment of the World: Israel*. Chicago: Children's Press, 1986.

Kalman, Bobbie. *The Lands, People, and Cultures Series: India the Culture*. New York: Crabtree Publishing Company, 1990.

McNair, Sylvia. *Enchantment of the World: India*. Chicago: Children's Press, 1990.

Nach, James. *England in Pictures*. Minneapolis, MN: Lerner Publications Company, 1990.

Patterson, Jose. *Country Fact Files: Israel*. Madison, NJ: Raintree/Steck-Vaughn, 1997.

Perrin, Penelope. *Discovering: Russia*. New York: Crestwood House, 1994.

Ramdin, Ron. *World in View: West Indies*. Madison, NJ: Raintree/Steck-Vaughn, 1991.

Sallnow, John. *Country Fact Files: Russia*. Madison, NJ: Raintree/Steck-Vaughn, 1997.

Steele, Philip. *Discovering: China*. New York: Crestwood House, 1994.

Thompson, Kathleen. *Portrait of America: Puerto Rico*. Madison, NJ: Raintree/Steck-Vaughn, 1996.

Torchinskii, Oleg. *Cultures of the World: Russia*. New York: Marshall Cavendish, 1994.

Waterlow, Julia. *Country Insights: China*. Madison, NJ: Raintree/Steck-Vaughn, 1997.

Video Tapes and CD-ROMs

AAA Travel Video Series: Puerto Rico. VHS. Wehman Video Distribution, 1995.

Discovering China and Tibet. VHS. Educational Filmstrip & Video, 1995.

Fodor's: Great Britain. VHS. International Video Network, 1992.

Great Metros: Beijing and Hong Kong. VHS. International Video Network, 1996.

Great Metros: London and Calcutta. VHS. International Video Network, 1996.

Van Arsdale, William G. *Best of the Caribbean: Handbook Companion, The*. VHS. Van Arsdales Video Travel, 1987.

Video Visits: *Discovering England*. VHS. International Video Network, 1993.

Vvafr, Shalom Sesame. *Land of Israel*. VHS. Baker & Taylor Video, 1988.

Vvafr, Shalom Sesame. *People of Israel*. VHS. Baker & Taylor Video, 1988.

Soyinka, Wole Vvsbc. *Voice of Africa*. VHS. Baker & Taylor Video, 1992.

3D Atlas Video Bundle. CD-ROM. Eakin Publications, 1996.

20th Century Video Almanac. CD-ROM. St. Louis City Art Museum, 1995.

World Wide Web Tourism Sites

Caribbean (West Indies) http://www.caribtourism.com

China http://www.chinatourpage.com

England http://www.visitbritain.com

India http://www.tourindia.com

Israel http://www.goisrael.com

Puerto Rico

http://Welcome.toPuertoRico.org

Russia http://www.tours.ru

South Africa

http://www.africa.com/captour/captour.htm

Embassy Addresses, Telephone Numbers, and Web Sites

England (United Kingdom)

3100 Massachusetts Avenue NW,
Washington, DC 20008.
(202) 462-1340.
http://www.britain-info.org

China

2300 Connecticut Avenue NW,
Washington, DC 20008.
(202) 328-2500.
http://www.china-embassy.org

India

2107 Massachusetts Avenue NW,
Washington, DC 20008.
(202) 939-7000.
http://www.indianembassy.org

Israel 3514 International Drive NW,
Washington, DC 20008.
(202) 364-5500.
http://www.israelemb.org

Puerto Rico (Chamber of Commerce)

100 Tetuan, P.O. Box S-3789,
San Juan, Puerto Rico 00902.
http://fortaleza.govpr.org or Puerto
Rico Federal Affairs Administration
http://www.prfaa-govpr.org

Russia

2650 Wisconsin Avenue NW,
Washington, DC 20007.
(202) 298-5700.
http://www.russianembassy.org

St. Vincent and the Grenadines

1717 Massachusetts Avenue NW,
Washington, DC 20036.

South Africa

3051 Massachusetts Avenue NW,
Washington, DC 20008.
(202) 232-4400.
http://www.southafrica.net

Index